ENDORSEM

Do you ever feel weary of "going through the motions" in your spiritual life? "Making a list and checking it twice" to be sure you've completed your spiritual exercises for the day? Have you ever wondered if you have done enough...or, if you *are* enough? If so, get ready to embark on a whole new journey. Joyful Intentionality is Allison Bown's guide to a living relationship with God that is vibrant, alive, fresh, utterly delightful, and exceedingly purposeful. You will be challenged to re-think some of your perceptions, and offered tools to reshape old mindsets about God, yourself, and the life He intends for you. This book will help you joyfully and happily pursue the treasure that's already inside...and enjoy the process.

— **Jane Hansen Hoyt**
President/CEO, Aglow International

Mindsets (the way we have learned or have been taught to think about things) have an enormous impact on the way we live and enjoy, or don't enjoy, life with God. Allison Bown effectively and humorously addresses new mindsets that invite us to engage the Lord and the life with which He gifted us with great joy, intentionality, anticipation and passion. She contrasts these renewed mindsets with the old ones that do not serve us well in our journey through life with Him. As I read, I laughed, I groaned and I completely agreed. Having spent over forty years in local church ministry I recommend this book to you with great enthusiasm! It will change how you think about God, how you think about yourself, and how you choose to live your life with Him.

— **Charles Patterson**
Founding Pastor of Church of the Hills
Austin, Texas

With a writing style that engages you from the first paragraph and content that is rich and enlightening, Allison Bown invites you to live your life with God from a place of freedom and joy. You won't find lists of "how-to's" or "you should haves," but instead she encourages the reader to develop a relationship with God that is motivated by love instead of one that is motivated by fear of punishment. This is a timely message for those who have discovered that the formulas never worked anyway.

— **Denise Siemens**
Founder/President, Arise! Women
Minneapolis, Minnesota

In these days of technological speed and microwave magic, Allison gives us an intriguing invitation to explore God's plans of purposeful and thoughtful development for our lives. Throughout Joyful Intentionality, you will find Allison's unique ability to give language to questions that have been stirring in your heart, insight into the process of spiritual growth and a fresh perspective of being changed into His image. This book will undoubtedly help you understand how Holy Spirit is using your practical, everyday circumstances as building blocks to mature you and connect you with God in greater intimacy. Allison has personally been on the journey of growing in perceiving God's involvement in her life in a way that is not fleeting but transformational. Joyful Intentionality is an opportunity to embrace God's intentional interaction in your own life in a way that will transform you and impact everyone around you. Be prepared to not merely gain knowledge of God's ways; be prepared to be transformed.

—**Mary Forsythe**
Founder/President of Kingdom Living Ministries
Author of *A Glimpse of Grace*

Allison is one of those people I can sit and converse with for hours; listening, responding, asking good questions, and then leave feeling so loved, valued and affirmed as one of Papa God's favorites. She is such a treasure to the Body of Christ, not just for her gift of encouragement, but because she writes with inspiration from the Father's heart. Her words soak deep into the reader, and there is a sense of "incarnation and embodiment"as each sentence jumps off of the page and pierces the heart with emotions that are hard to articulate. I kept reading the same pages over and over again, feeling more secure in my connection with Papa God, and learning how to rest in His love for me. More than that, she is writing with the intent that what the reader is receiving goes beyond encouragement, and is transformational, changing the way we do life! So powerful and highly recommended!!

—**Mike Horn**
Pastor, Student, Life-long Learner
Sacramento, California

Joyful Intentionality promises to inspire and challenge readers to think with the mind of Christ. Allison Bown is full of integrity, passion, creativity and purpose, all of which flow onto these pages. There is no way to read this book and not be transformed.

—**Judith MacNutt**
President/Co-founder, Christian Healing Ministries
Jacksonville, Florida

Allison has been an inspiration and precious friend to me for many years. Together, we shared God's love to incarcerated women in the prisons of California and witnessed their miracles of new life for over fifteen years. Although we were not the usual evangelists called into this mission field, the women knew we understood their joy! God had set us free from religious bondages and partnered with us as vessels in His process of freedom for them. It has been my privilege to walk with Jesus for over seventy years and I will always treasure my journey with Allison as "delightful traveling days." In her wonderful new book, she shares many of the lessons that God has taught her along the way. As only she can do, Allison will cause you to smile, expand your vision, and create a fresh desire to walk with God...with purpose and joy!

— **Earlene Leming**
Founding member of California Aglow Prison Ministry/
Leadership Development
Author of *Vessels of Honor* books

This book is fun. The idea of a joyful intentionality as we approach life is the childlike anticipation of the first day of a new school year, an anticipated weekend with the family at Disneyland, and the rising early on Christmas morning. But to fulfill the joy means to not stand at the gate of the school and watch as other students line up, or standing at the gate of Disneyland and watching others go through the turnstile, or sitting on the stairs looking at the presents through the rails, it means actually going in, participating, and fulfilling your joy. So, in anticipation of partnering with God in life, we read, go to a conference, and even study to experience not only the collection of information, but the actualization of transformation. Allison sets the course, with a mindset of intentionality we enter the arena for life-change, not just another information transaction. How you approach something will determine what you receive. Joy is anchored in eternity, and it works. Your attitude shapes your aptitude and your receptors so that the joyful intake of the things of God move you past data into destiny. When you approach life's learning experiences with joy, everything matters and you change. Thanks Allison.

— **Gary Goodell**
Author of *Permission Granted to do Church Differently in the 21st Century*
and *Where Would Jesus Lead?*

I have the absolute delight of calling Allison my friend. Time and again I have enjoyed the joyful intentionality with which she approaches every circumstance and all of life. Anyone who knows Allison knows that she has a gift for words. She has a rich language that communicates Kingdom principles in a way that enables you to live them out in your own life. As you read Joyful Intentionality, you will experience Allison's artful ability to stand in a moment, absorb every bit of truth from it, live it out in her own life and communicate it to the reader. The process is what makes us rich and this book will help you to mine the treasures that make you wealthy.

—**Jenny Taylor**
Personal Assistant to Graham Cooke

It is my great privilege to know Allison as a friend and fellow adventurer in the Kingdom. She is one of the most joyfully intentional people I know. Being in her company always encourages and challenges me to dive deeper into the "passion driven life with God...on purpose," this book describes. Joyful Intentionality is not just a good read. It is also an authentic distillation of Allison's real life journey with God. It will inspire you to experience the depths of love God has for you. It will guide you to discover the boundless joyful intentionality that is the basis of all God's thoughts and actions toward you. It will give you the tools to mine the riches that can only be found in the "process" of the relationship God is relentlessly pursuing with each of us. This book is a banquet to be savored and as you feast on the truth served here, the Holy Spirit will empower you to explore your own life of Joyful Intentionality.

—**Bob Book**
www.bobbookmusic.com

JOYFUL
INTENTIONALITY

A PASSION-FILLED LIFE
ON PURPOSE

ALLISON
BOWN

Brilliant
BOOK HOUSE

This book and other materials published by Allison Bown are available online at www.BrilliantBookHouse.com

Published by Brilliant Book House
PO BOX 871450
Vancouver, WA, 98687

Unless otherwise indicated, all Scripture quotation are taken from New King James Version.

If you would like more information on Allison Bown, please visit www.twclass.org.

ISBN: 978-0-9896262-3-1

To my truly amazing mother,
Jerrie Lopez Miller,
a friend of God.

You have been my faithful champion in this life,
my best cheerleader and chief conspirator in mischief.

You are a ripple effect of God's goodness in this world,
and the words on these pages contain a great deal of your impact,
as do the lives of all whom you have loved.

The Father has done exceedingly, abundantly beyond all
we could have asked or thought.

But then...you always knew that He would.

ACKNOWLEDGEMENTS

No one writes a book in isolation, and this one is infused with the kindness, grace and wisdom of many of my family and friends:

My husband Randy, who is my steady, patient and wise counsel. My best friend for thirty years who keeps me focused on what really matters, and my partner in fun. Together, we speak our own language of promise, encouragement, and "Seinfeld." I am profoundly grateful for the freedom to fly and the home base that we share.

My friend and personal assistant, Teresa Morrison. You are a true Joseph, a faithful steward of our business, a champion encourager and visionary. You expertly launch the new members of The Warrior Class, and your wise eye on our finances has probably saved us from the certain ruin of my inability to do math (or tendency to leave the bank bag laying about…somewhere…).

To the members of The Warrior Class and our pioneering Leadership Roundtable: You are fearless, fabulous and fun! Together, we are redefining the concepts of warfare, training, and intercession to become joyful, invigorating, and renewing. You guys rock!

Theresa Cooke, who firmly put her arm into mine and swept me into a world that is expansive and delightful. You fill every room you enter with life. Thank you for being my fierce friend, champion and savvy chief of all things "Cooke."

Jenny Taylor is the "Queen of Everything" at Brilliant Perspectives and my hero of friendship. You *see me*.

To the mob at Brilliant Book House: you are pure awesomeness. Mark, Sophie, Sheila and Sarah, you make excellence look cool.

Bob Book, you've sung the soundtrack for my life for over a decade, and who you are in worship continues to challenge me to become a magnificent minister to the Lord above all else. And Barb, thanks for always being sure to know where I am. I'm certain that, without your trusty eye, I would be aimlessly wandering about Mongolia.

Thanks to Byron and Crystal Easterling, whom I think are fairly sure that I live at their house.

To Kelly Megonigle, my friend who brilliantly captains my personal intercessors. I'm so glad we survived the "Street of Death" in Vancouver, WA those many years ago.

To all those who took the time to read this manuscript in its various incarnations, who gave genius ideas, proofread, and prayed: thank you. And double thanks to Veronica Mahaffey, whose expert editor's eyes let my style soar while giving it professional excellence.

To my Aglow Prison Ministry moms, Earlene Leming and Rachel Bondshu, who have faithfully prayed, listened, cheered, and empowered me for almost two decades: may I one day be half the champions that you are.

And to my friend, brother and chief partner in exploration, Graham Cooke: we've journeyed from acquaintance-hood, through "Obi-Wan/ Skywalker" days and into a collaboration that would make Lewis & Clark proud.

You've graciously said many times that what you had was mine to use, and you will certainly see your DNA reflected in these pages. Hopefully I've been faithful to your one condition: that when I had made it better (with the confident tone of "You can…and you will"), it would become yours to borrow back.

I think that what is here is unique, rather than better — another lens on truth with infinite facets to explore. But I believe there are a few nuggets that you'll find worth taking. I hope so. Both you and Jesus deserve an excellent return on your investment of grace, wisdom, patience and kindness in my life.

Calling people up into their truest Kingdom identity is not just a nice teaching that you do. It is truly who you are.

Contents

PART 1
KEY MINDSETS OF JOYFULLY INTENTIONAL PEOPLE

PART 2
BUILDING A JOYFULLY INTENTIONAL LIFE WITH GOD

PART 3
QUESTIONS AND CONSIDERATIONS FOR PERSONAL PROCESS

FOREWORD — *by Graham Cooke*

"To count everything as joy" is an extraordinary permission. To put joy at the forefront of any life experience that involves trials, testing endurance, developing maturity and learning wisdom (James 1:2-8) is a stroke of absolute genius!

Joy creates a faith focus that eliminates even the slight possibility of being in two minds. Joy stabilizes our inner equilibrium so that trust can concentrate on the nature of God. He lives in everlasting joy. He is the happiest person I know. He has the sunniest disposition of anyone I have ever met in life. There is laughter in His eyes, music in His words, good cheer in the detail of His planning for us (John 16:33). Joy gives us courage to stand because it opens our heart to the fullness of God's loving purpose, where we relax into His smile over us.

God is always the same, yesterday, today and forever. He is unchanging in His nature. He is untroubled, undisturbed, un-agitated, unflappable, unworried. He is the best person with whom to do life. He is peaceful, calm, composed, steady, tranquil, and cool. Laughter is never very far from the surface of His innate goodness. It bubbles underneath His fixed and ready focus like a strong running underground stream of refreshing life-giving water.

Placing joy as a tipping point in all our life circumstances empowers us to receive His presence no matter what is occurring. Joy and strength; rejoicing and resolution; thanksgiving and fortitude; exulting and courage; gladness and boldness; celebration and fearlessness; cheerful and tough. Always study the contrasts in scripture…" Be of good cheer, I have overcome."

A happy person will be secure enough to risk. God is consistent but unpredictable. We always know where we are in His Nature, but we seldom know where we are in His actions. In Himself He is unchanging. Pick an aspect of His nature and focus on it for a few moments. Love, joy, peace, patience, goodness, kindness, gentleness, grace, mercy, courage, boldness, fearlessness, etc. They are all constants. Fixed, firm, continual, and faithful. He gives Himself to us and thereby becomes The Rock of our very experience.

His actions require faith. His nature requires the trust of a much-loved child. A child will take a leap of faith where an adult would defer. Joy is the difference in fighting well or not fighting at all.

Allison is a warrior. Happy in battle, great in confrontation, and even-tempered in a crisis. She has the thousand-yard stare of someone who knows focus. Underneath everything is a delightful sense of fun, underpinned by good cheer and the captivating hard work of enjoyment in Jesus. It is a pleasure to walk with God. We must work as hard on our pleasures as we must on our calling. To have the latter without the former makes us dull and lacking in astonishment.

Allison is a brilliant trainer. Like all excellent presenters of truth, she doesn't just pick up on the precepts but listens to the underlying values in relationship. Fellowship is an amazing learning environment. We learn the best in a state of togetherness.

When you read or listen to my friend Al, you will hear Jesus laughing in the wings. He will be tapping His foot to the melody of grace and truth. You will feel His eyes on you, and when you look into the warmth of His smile you will feel His gaze of joyful intentionality.

People who walk with God radiate His presence. It's the mix of the message in the messenger that shouts abroad the freedom and the permission of the One who turns slaves into sons. You'll read that on the pages of this book. The heart of the Father will touch you, and as you partner with the always jubilant Holy Spirit, the Lord Jesus will become more real to you.

I recommend this book not because I like Al's writing (though I sincerely do!) but because I know her spirit. I know the tune that God plays on her heart. I've sung that song myself. It's the melody of joyful intentionality. This book creates opportunities for you to explore and discover God. It's a map and the Holy Spirit is your compass.

Travel well and...arrive!

Graham Cooke
www.brilliantperspectives.com

A PRAYER AS YOU READ:

*Father, we are outrageously grateful that when you imagined life with us,
it was with joy, delight, passion and permission.*

*You wrote all our days in Your book before time ever was and
we are now learning to read the story of our lives with You.
Thank You, that as we read, we encounter our journey as You have written it.*

*We rejoice that the eternal sacrifice of Jesus erases all the places where our
adversary has tried to pencil in a false tale of lack, fear and performance to earn
the love that You so freely give.*

*You are the great and abundant Gift Giver.
We are becoming Champion Receivers.*

*Holy Spirit, do what You do so beautifully. Sit with us as we read Your story of
us and the words written here. Craft what we hear into a unique encounter with
You as our Teacher, Helper, Comforter and Friend.*

*We are so thankful that You continually connect us to the Mind of Christ
and the Heart of the Father, that we may become the Body that Jesus deserves;
running without fear, in outstanding joy, into all You have prepared for us.*

*So that the world would know how good You really are
and how beloved we were all created to be.*

*In Jesus name,
Amen*

PREFACE:
FREEDOM FROM "COMPETITIVE EATING CHRISTIANITY"

The last day at any great conference has a familiar feel. You have a sense of having been transported into another realm with God. Your notebook is bulging, and you exchange email addresses with the new friends you've made. Then there's the mad dash to the book table to gather all the resources you can in an attempt to bring this mountaintop feeling home with you, back into your everyday life.

It was on one of those last days that I found myself halfway across a church parking lot, getting ready to depart, arms full of books and CDs. Suddenly, I was acutely aware of God's presence. I could feel Him peacefully wrapping His arms around me from behind...and He had something to say.

Was it going to be another great revelation on the topic of the conference?

Was it going to be an expression of thanks for taking time off from work to come to this event?

Instead, it was a series of whispered questions, gently asked with love and challenge.

> **"How many conferences, Allison? How many CDs?
> How many books have you read?"**

I stopped in my tracks. I didn't know. It was a lot...a *whole* lot. Hundreds for sure. Thousands? Possibly. I had been raised in church, attended Christian schools, camps, and universities. I had been a Sunday School teacher, a choir director, a short-term missionary, and was currently volunteering in a women's prison ministry.

But those questions were only a warm up. He was about to get to His main point:

"How many of them have you actually become?"

Uhhh... I'd never thought of it that way. I had certainly grown in the Lord over the years, but I also still worried a lot, was very self-conscious and insecure. Yet...surely, most of what I had heard had taken root. It had to have. Didn't it?

As I drove home, I began to think more deeply about the amazing conference I had just experienced. I tried to make a mental list of the profound truths that I had spent three days listening to, but the list was short. I had cheered, applauded, and been deeply moved, but I was already beginning to forget. Wait! That's why I had taken notes, right? Then I realized: I couldn't remember the last time I had reviewed my notes from a conference...any conference. When I tried to recall life-changing thoughts from the last meetings I'd attended and books I'd read, I soberly understood:

Volume had not equaled maturity.
Just hearing about God hadn't transformed me into being like Him.

The initial pain of that revelation revealed why God approached me with such kindness—so that I would not mistake His inquiries for judgment. His gentle tone made it clear that He wasn't mad or disappointed. How could He be? He already knew what I was just discovering. It was simply time for us to have a conversation so that I would understand it, too.

In the weeks that followed, I began to discover just how much of my security and sense of identity was rooted in my performance, rather than in who God said I was. I was living with the weight of our relationship carried mostly on my shoulders, always trying to be who I thought God wanted me to be. The Father was kindly revealing that my life was more about how much I did than Who I knew, more centered on working for acceptance than on receiving the truth that I was accepted in the Beloved.

In my self-generated efforts to be good enough, I had missed the truth of Philippians 2:13: "God is working in you, giving you the desire to obey Him and the power to do what pleases Him."

**God initiates His work in us.
Desire for obedience is His *gift*,
wrapped in the power to do what delights Him.**

Gifts are made to be received, not earned. What child races out to the tree on Christmas morning, only to stop in their tracks to consider if they've behaved well enough to deserve their presents? What kid in their right mind would double check with their parents to be sure that the amount of presents they were receiving was equivalent to the chores they had performed in the past twelve months? Children are excellent receivers of gifts. If a present is present, they don't question that the decision to give it has already been made...and they'll take it!

As children of God, our role is not to generate obedience, but it is to cultivate a life that receives the desire to obey and walks actively in the power God gives us to do what delights Him. The source of our desire to obey God? Love. "If anyone loves Me, keep My words" (John 14:23). Obedience was meant to grow out of our being overwhelmed by His first love for us, our desire to keep His words the natural overflow of being so astonishingly adored.

Overwhelmed and overflowing...in that order.

Giving gifts is an intentional action; when it's prompted by passion, it's such a joy. Of course you want to give back to the One who has so lavishly given to you! Obedience from love is living and light. Obedience from obligation or fear of God's disapproval or disappointment is a heavy, heavy burden.

That day in the parking lot, I would have enthusiastically agreed with every statement you just read. However, the reality of my life was that I was still trying so hard to love Jesus by working to get our relationship *just right*, yet always feeling that it never quite was. I was reading all the books, listening to all the talks, and doing everything I felt I was supposed to do to be a "good Christian"...and I was exhausted. I was overfed and undernourished. I had gorged on teaching and how-to's, but in my honest moments, I rarely felt at rest or that God was deeply satisfied with me.

vii

COMPETITIVE EATING VS. FINE DINING

My first light bulb moment following my parking lot encounter came a few weeks later. It was the 4th of July. I was flipping through the TV channels and I happened upon the annual broadcast of the famous Coney Island Hot Dog Eating Contest — the Superbowl of professional, competitive eating.

And I realized that I was looking in a mirror.

I saw for the first time that out of my mistaken mindset of "more equals maturity" I had inadvertently become a Christian Competitive Eating Champion, trained to spread resources out before me like the hot dogs that were neatly stacked in front of each Coney Island competitor. An imaginary whistle blew in my head, and I gobbled teachings, CDs, and books as quickly as I could. I obtained a weird satisfaction in how much I consumed, and it didn't occur to me to consider if any of it was being properly digested. Speed and volume were what drew applause from the crowd, and look: medals were being given to the champion! That felt good to me...for a little while.

But spiritually, what was I becoming a champion of? A report card? An exam? Having interesting facts to add to an academic conversation? Just as a hot dog eating contest is not a true representation of how (or what) humans were created to eat, neither is gobbling mass quantities of Christian teaching the way we were meant to ingest the true milk and meat of the Kingdom.

My old mindsets continued to be dismantled as I reflected on my experiences of "time with God" at church every Sunday morning. A defining pattern began to emerge of how I expected to connect with God:

Enter.

Sing.

Sit.

Listen.

Respond (if asked).

Exit the building.

Repeat fifty-two times a year.

And if I forgot what was said? No worries, because there was a new teaching coming in seven days—or even sooner if I also attended Sunday night and mid-week services. If I did that, my menu of fifty-two different messages a year ballooned to an even more ridiculous number!

No one can digest that much!

And imagine life for the precious ministers who also live with the expectation of this pattern. Frankly, can any chef prepare that many memorable meals in a row? No wonder "fast food" teaching has emerged in the church: minimal prep time supplemented by lots of advertising for tasty bites that feel good in the moment but are contributing minimally to a healthy, continual growth process. It's an overwhelming challenge for leaders to develop gourmet spiritual meals when many people have become used to the fast pace of competitive Christian eating.

And I was a champion of this lifestyle...*for years*, simply because I had not experienced anything else, nor had it occurred to me to think that there might be something different. It's not that it wasn't out there, but until that day in the parking lot, it hadn't been part of my experience.

Truth, like real food, was created to be savored and to be expertly paired with the fine, aged wine of Wisdom, sipped slowly.

Quality, preparation, and presentation are meant to be carefully considered in partnership with the Master Chef, whether you are cooking with Him or are dining as His guest, hosted by a friend who's spent considerable time in His kitchen. Like all the best dinner experiences with good friends, conversation around the table unfolds in layers as each skillfully prepared course builds on the one before it. And when the gloriously long evening finally comes to a close, everyone present has spent a memorable time together.

Meals like that stand out to us because we don't have them every day and because of their excellence. Long after the food has been finished, we still savor the experience. Several weeks after attending such a meal, you may be having coffee with some of your fellow guests when someone begins to recount the evening. As each friend reminisces with the group about their favorite dish and the seasonings they loved, you watch their countenance change as they blissfully recall what made that evening so special for them. Shared memories momentarily transport everyone back to that evening—until the moment is interrupted by the beep of a text notification from someone's cell phone. Your friend checks their phone and happily announces, "Hey everyone! We've been invited back! The Master Chef and his friend want to teach us how to make every one of those dishes ourselves!" Suddenly everyone buzzes with excitement, reaching for phones & agendas to clear their calendars for that evening, energetically talking over each other as they share which dish they want to learn to make first.

This is the kind of experience God intended for us. All He has ever wanted from us is a vibrant, personal relationship with us. He desires friends to sit together at His feast table, sharing the experience—not just servants who bring in the food and leave (John 15:15). His heart's desire has always been for us to take what we've encountered and partner with the Holy Spirit to cultivate initial truth into our living reality. From the overflow of that lifestyle, we naturally share with others, offering them an opportunity to taste and see the feast of goodness, kindness and graciousness that God has so lavishly shared with us (Psalm 34:8).

Consider how many occasions in scripture were set at a dinner table or involved meals: Passover and the numerous feasts of the Old Testament; Jesus' first miracle at the wedding feast in Cana where He turned the water into wine; His evening spent eating with His disciples that we know as the "Last Supper." Twice, Jesus was anointed with fragrant oil as He was sitting at a dinner table, and He was often in trouble with the Pharisees for having too much fun while dining. Jesus even did a bit of cooking Himself following His resurrection, frying up some fish so His friends could have breakfast. Many of the stories He told are built around the imagery of meals. In Luke 14:23, Jesus declares clearly that His feast table will be full. At times, His version of a perfect atmosphere for eating may seem odd to us: apparently, being surrounded by people who want to kill you serves as a perfect setting to sit down and dine. ("You prepare a table before me in the presence of my enemies....")

Psalm 23:5) Whatever the context, meals seem to be a parable for life that God is very fond of using.

In the natural, people who prepare fine food are passionate about what they do in a way that the fry cook at the local Burger Palace is presumably not. The hours they spend designing, shopping, and creating gourmet meals are a delight, not an obligation. And the friends who reap the benefits of their passion not only respond to dinner invitations with delight but arrive full of expectancy, happy to be there, and glad to take their time to enjoy every moment. When the chef is also a brilliant teacher, the grand finale is not only a decadent dessert but includes an invitation for guests to come back again in order to learn how to prepare the meal for themselves and to share it with others!

Both the preparer and consumer share a passion for excellent food, and that enthusiasm is what motivates them. Speed and convenience are not high priorities. Reading a gourmet recipe without actually creating it is unthinkable: they don't want to just hear that it's great or memorize the ingredients. They want to experience that spectacular dish for themselves, even if it takes repeated practice to learn. Being motivated by passion, engaging in the learning process is not a question of discipline or work, but rather an adventurous opportunity too good to pass up because the resulting rewards of a choice meal and great fellowship are so wonderful.

That's Joyful Intentionality:
A passion-driven life with God...on purpose...because it is so worth it.

If "joyful" is separated from "intentionality" — if "purpose" precedes "passion" — then our spirituality can quickly turn into a duty to be done, not a relational process to be savored. The joy of life with God can elude us if we don't intimately know in Whom we have believed and are absolutely assured that He is well able to care for every detail of our lives (2 Timothy 1:12). We will forget that trust must essentially be connected with our learning, because learning does not always guarantee understanding (Isaiah 55:9).

When we connect with the passion that God has for and extends to us, we remain fervent friends of His who are motivated by desire — not merely disciplined employees afraid of reprimand. It becomes our good pleasure to take personal responsibility for developing our lives with Him, learning the process of preparation because we simply enjoy being with Him. We take on His character of thoughtful consideration about what will best fuel us for the next part of our journey. Life shifts from being about what we are going to do and becomes about Who we are doing it with.

The religious alternative to an authentic relationship with God is a work-driven, behaviorally-based system that requires us to continually prove our progress. It develops checklists ("10 Steps to…" and "30 Day Transformation Tips…") to measure and evaluate our apparent spiritual growth. While these may hold some helpful information, they're too often formulas that imply, "Do these steps and you will become this." They can eliminate our dependency on the Holy Spirit and delay the discovery of our unique identity and story which are found in Christ as we journey with Him and with others.

In our spirituality, it's a challenge at times to choose quality over convenience, much as it is in the natural to resist the allure of the numerous fast food options that offer to rescue us from the process of shopping, preparation and cooking that good food requires. We fall into a routine:

Ate veggies? Check. (French fries are a vegetable, right?)

Drank soda? Check. (Which is a liquid, so my thirst should be quenched.)

Consumed dubiously identified meat product? Check.

Full? Check.

Done in four minutes and thirty seconds? Check. (Would've finished sooner if the server wasn't taking so much time with the customer in front of me….)

In search of a quick break-through, we can "drive through," pick up our self-help book, make a checklist, quantify our progress and move on. Consumption has occurred; but nutrition is questionable and eating on the run rarely involves quality fellowship.

**Joyful Intentionality understands that breakthroughs are appetizers.
Follow-through is the main course.**

In comparison, a Joyfully Intentional life is a gloriously long, delectable meal that is highly relational and features the savory intangibles of passion, trust and faith. Every encounter or revelation becomes the beginning of a sumptuous process, not an obligation to be completed as quickly as possible.

ENJOYING A GOURMET MEAL

The day that God challenged me in the parking lot rocked my world. As I've travelled in ministry, I've heard the cry of my heart echoed in countless conversations: "I don't want just one more conference, good book, or CD set. I want to live the life the teaching talks about!"

My friend and chief partner-in-exploration, Graham Cooke, has relentlessly pursued the personal cultivation of a gourmet relationship with God that has given us 5-Star resources to develop our own brilliant lives with Him. In 2010, Graham & I began pioneering in the Kingdom together, from which The Warrior Class (TWC) has emerged—a passionate team of men and women training together on the battleground of prophetic intercession. As TWC has grown, I've come to realize that we are actually living a Joyfully Intentional life—not just talking about one.

Our members are learning how to explore more with less, taking a handful of materials and a significant amount of time (8-12 months) to digest them. We provide a buffet of options so that they can partner with the Holy Spirit in creating their own unique process of development. Instead of an exam to demonstrate comprehension, we ask for "Evidences of Transformation" (Tell us how you've become what you've been beholding in the areas of thinking, language, faith, works and more.) The testimonies are amazing!

We've been able to practice our encounters on the training ground and battlefield of prophetic intercession, so all of our learning has real-world experience to go with it. We're not just reading a recipe book. We're creating the meals! And though we may be physically spread far and wide across the globe, we have developed a spiritual community of friends that is dynamic and encouraging because we share common passions.

(Visit www.twclass.org to learn more about The Warrior Class.)

It shouldn't work. Our application process is not simple. We are not a come one, come all community. We strongly value allowing prospective members to try on our style and focus to see if it fits for them. It's not for everyone, and that's okay. We're specialists! Our Kingdom assignments are very specific, and we steadfastly stay within the parameters of what we are called to do. We welcome fellow travelers who share the same calling and passions, and gladly bless those who discover that TWC is not for them at this time. Knowing who we are and what we are created to do frees us from having to do it all (an old mindset that I am very grateful to be released from).

The Warrior Class is pioneering a new type of prophetic intercession. Often we're running to keep up with all that we are discovering, but there are rarely complaints. Because very few of our members live in close proximity to another member, our fellowship is largely virtual. But when we do gather together, the room hums with excitement, laughter and brilliance. We share a passionate purpose, and that purpose has produced joyful, resilient warriors and intercessors who love life in the "clash between the two Kingdoms" — the Kingdom of God and the king- dom of evil. We're not just gathering to talk about someone else's discov- eries. We're eagerly sharing our own!

And almost every single one of us has intentionally travelled a steep, uphill climb out of our competitive eating and fast food spiritual mind- sets with our hearts set on exploring the heights of passionate relation- ship with the Father. The very nature of our process has brought us into conflict, where we've been given opportunity to choose either advance- ment in the joy of relational process or a return to the task master of performance. Religion taught us to think in terms of rules and standards that we *have to* meet for acceptance, but we've discovered that Jesus offers a uniquely personal kinship, sharing His love with us and making obedience and holiness something we gladly want to do because we are His friends (John 14:23).

Over time, we've equipped our spiritual kitchen with tools and ingredi- ents that allow us to create memorable feasts with our wonderful Friend, the Master Chef. As we discover our inherent identity as both warriors and intercessors, we find that we covet the preferred seating of His table, set in the presence of our enemies. Together we've enjoyed many tasty meals cooked up by both TWC leaders and members on the battlefield. Sure, we've had a few smoky experiments as we're learning, but the quality of our results continues to grow steadily. We certainly enjoy the love and laughter we share around His table, just as we relish being fiercely focused on the exquisite fight that is our priority.

We know that God hasn't reserved this Joyfully Intentional life for only The Warrior Class or any one group of people. We've met lots of fellow sojourners in our travels who are exploring their Kingdom possibilities. Just like God graciously stopped me that day in the parking lot, He is looking for creative ways to take all of us to a new level of relationship with Him and enjoy the journey together.

NAVIGATING THIS BOOK

This book is a guide for your unique story with God: a source of possibilities for you to explore, rather than a workbook to be completed. The concepts and ideas presented are meant to provide ingredients that will allow you to begin to create your own brilliant feast with Jesus. It's not intended as a recipe to follow without deviation. It's more like the times I spent as a child cooking with my Nana: the ingredients will vary in proportion as the Father measures them from the palm of His hand rather than an exact measuring spoon—and the outcome will be delicious!

THE PURPOSE OF "QUESTIONS FOR EXPLORATION"

There are a handful of "Questions for Exploration" at the end of Chapters 1-7 for you to take notes on. They are not there to measure your comprehension of the content but rather to provoke fresh thoughts and personal connections. There is a space for you to record your reflections so far—because you are not giving a final answer but are beginning a process of contemplation. You will find that what you write during your first reading may be quite different than what you will see the next time through or after you discuss it further with others. That is the nature of a living process.

However, that may not have been your life experience in how questions are used. The world's system of learning usually asks questions as proof of mastery and completion.

**Our history with answering questions in these environments
may have equated the concept of questions with a sense
anxiety or fear of failure.**

Consider the average classroom: it's a Q&A minefield for disaster. To
begin with, you only had a one in twenty chance (or less, depending on
the number of students) of being chosen by the teacher. That means, the
odds of success were already very slim. If you beat those odds, got your
hand up quickly and were called upon, then you had to actually have
the correct answer (questions in these settings usually only have one
right answer, so the pressure is on). If you answered incorrectly, then
you experienced the public humiliation of having the wrong answer in
front of all your friends. If you are someone that is more introverted in
your nature, even if you had the correct answer, you may have struggled
to find the words to accurately express it. And if by some miracle, you
achieved all of the above, the reward is short-lived. Your success was
acknowledged briefly, the next question was asked and the minefield
was entered again.

In traditional learning environments, once the questions are answered
correctly (either in a group discussion or at the end of a study guide),
it's usually time to move on to new material. We have tangible proof
of our knowledge, which is highly valued on report cards and certifi-
cates. Whether we mean to or not, we often bring this mindset into our
spiritual development. We may mistakenly believe that success is about
having one right answer (and having it quickly); about filling in a blank
or completing a quiz. And in doing so, we focus primarily on learning
what to think, rather than how to think.

**In the Kingdom, questions are asked to initiate
a process of exploration.**

Jesus asked well over a hundred questions in the Gospels; yet He only
gave or received direct answers to a few of them. He obviously wasn't
asking His questions to determine comprehension but to provoke listeners to think for themselves. Even when He inquired of His disciples,
"Who do people say that I am?" He didn't correct the wrong answers
they initially gave. He simply waited. Then He asked them to think for
themselves, "Who do YOU say that I am?" (Matthew 16:13-17).

If, after He had waited, they'd had no response, He may well have moved on to another topic. But that day, Peter did get the answer--and he got it in the same way that we do: through revelation. "Flesh and blood did not reveal this to you Peter, but My Father in Heaven…" (Matthew 16:17). Revelation may come in an instant, like Peter's did or it may come in bits and pieces over time (often out of sequence), requiring us to collect and treasure the pieces as they emerge. But no matter how it occurs, revelation is a starting point, not a finish line. It will need a Joyfully Intentional process of exploration in partnership with the Holy Spirit.

God does not use questions to check our comprehension. He uses them as tools to provoke our thinking and embark on a continuing path of discovery. The verbs used in Matthew 7:7 are progressive: "Ask—and keep on asking. Seek—and keep on seeking. Knock—and keep on knocking." Why? Is God trying to be elusive? No, He desires for us to enter into a process, not a program. He wants a relational conversation that continues to expand; going wider, higher and deeper as we travel with Him…

because life in the Kingdom is about Evidences of Transformation, not comprehension of material.

How has your perception of God's true identity been upgraded?

What brilliant God-thoughts are you having now that you didn't have before?

How does your every day language reflect more of His truth?

What actions are you taking now that reflect your new perspective?

What specific aspects of your faith have grown stronger?

What has emerged more clearly in your own persona (how Heaven sees you and who God made you to truly be)?

These are questions of exploration that demonstrate our Evidences of Transformation: authentic indicators of having lived in a truth until you have begun to become it. Each "Evidence" will have a story: a real-life example from your journey that confirms that this is no longer just what you know, but truly who you are becoming.

For many people, just the sight of questions evokes a fear of getting a wrong answer. If you are one of those, then I have good news: there are no test questions here, only tools to encourage you to pause, consider and explore. Use the questions and the activations in this book as resources for your own, continual discovery process with God.

They are a compass—not a quiz.

PART 1: MINDSETS

The first part of this book focuses on the mindsets of a Joyfully Intentional life. "As a man thinks in his heart, so is he"(Proverbs 23:7). Unless we learn to share God's Divine perspective, even the best spiritual ingredients will not mix well and will not produce the maturity and abundant life that He has promised to us. How we perceive and think about God is always our starting place. The initial chapters are written to immerse you in the mindsets, language and actions of Joyfully Intentional people walking with God. It will give you a sense of what this lifestyle looks like and will allow you to consider what upgrades you want to pursue in your growth process.

PART 2: TOOLS

The second part of the book will give you ideas for exploration. It is like opening a pantry or tool room: it offers lots of choices and options that you can mix, match, and expand upon to create your own Joyfully Intentional relationship with God. It is important to not only understand the ways of God through study but to also have experiences with truth that create a relationship with God that is authentic, not theoretical. The activations and ideas included are a few of the ways I've discovered that effectively open up spaces for encounters that lead to true transformation.

They are creative ways of being with God…not more things to do for Him.

PART 3: RESOURCES

Finally, there is a Resource Section that goes beyond "Questions for
Exploration." This section gives you tools, dialogue starters, and ways to
activate the provision that God has for each of your mindset upgrades.

These are additional ways for you to behold and become more of what
you're reading about (2 Corinthians 3:18). And whether you are reading
this book on your own or gathering with a small group to process what
you've read together, this section will offer you ways to explore your
journey.

With all my heart, I believe that it is not what we do that will last, but
who we become with God and each other that will have eternal signifi-
cance. When we are overwhelmed only by Who, then the what, where, &
how becomes an overflow of the Divine "yes" that we say and keep on
saying.

You have your own memorable feast to create—not for God, but with
Him and others.

INTRODUCTION:
BRIDGING THE GAP

"The gap between aspiration and achievement is called development."
- Graham Cooke

I love listening to people who dream, to men and women who can imagine something great. Whether based on a prophetic word they've received or Divine inspiration, it delights me to hear what they believe is possible. And, by the end of our conversation, their dream is often easy to visualize. They've painted a picture of the vision so vividly that it's easy to believe that they will attain their goals. Yet, for many people, their dream never manifests. Why is that?

Over the years, I've watched as some people's aspirations materialized, while others fizzled; several took flight and others flopped. I've seen tremendous opportunities become available but not be acted on. A number of people did amazing exploits with relatively little, while others who seemed to possess an abundance of resources haven't moved forward. I've known folks who received powerful prophecies, yet appear to remain stuck in their life's situations and circumstances, while those with seemingly less spectacular words have manifested change and incredibly impacted the lives of those around them. What made the difference?

Before all else we must consider the matter of timing. Timing is a piece of the puzzle that is completely in God's hands. He is in charge of both the outcome and the preparation of the path that takes us to our dream. Often, we feel He is either too late or moving too fast. However, though His ways are higher than ours; often beyond our understanding (Isaiah 55:8-9), when the timing and outcomes in our story are left in God's hands, we can trust and be at peace.

But what is our part in who we become? When God has shared His vision, given His promises of provision, and paved the way—is that it? Is our destiny and development like a motorized walkway in an airport? Once the image has been painted on our hearts, do we just step on and wait to arrive at the grand outcome?

PARABLES OF PROCESS

Jesus' stories of the Hidden Treasure and the search for the Pearl of Great Price have become a compass for me as I've explored these questions. Though they have a broader meaning, these scriptures are now my personal parables of process.

"The kingdom of heaven is like a treasure, hidden in a field, which a man found and hid; and for joy over it, he goes and sells all he has and buys that field" (Matthew 13:44). In the story of the Hidden Treasure, I see a man who is surprised by a sudden encounter of riches. He didn't plan to find a treasure, but once he discovered one, he didn't simply settle for the joy of discovery. He took the steps necessary to make the treasure authentically his.

A dishonest man would have grabbed the goods and ran. But this man embarks on the process to make the treasure his own. He is willing to pay a price for it (investing time and effort in the purchase) because he knows when the process is finished, the treasure will be his to do with as he sees fit. That makes his work to obtain it joyful! When he's completed the legal steps required for ownership, he can legitimately invest and expand his riches, spend it, or bless others with it.

When viewing this story through the lens of intentionality, I see Jesus showing us how to turn an unexpected Kingdom encounter or prophetic word from a great A-ha! moment into a truth that will be life-giving for many years to come. We can hear someone else's revelation (or even have a genuine personal experience with God), but if we just scoop it up and dash off to share it with others, it isn't really ours yet.

It's something that we know, but it's not yet become authentically who we are.

For authenticity, we often need to keep the illuminated truth we've learned hidden in our heart while we joyfully pursue the process of making it our own through meditation, prayer, scriptural exploration, and having our new-found revelation tested in times of adversity. How does our new revelation hold up in times of pressure to doubt? Has our concept transitioned from being another refrigerator magnet phrase that we admire into a rock-solid, foundational reality in our relationship with God?

That transition process may cost us in time, finances or the seeming loss of eminent opportunities. But we embrace the price of process with joy because we know that the end result is that we will be able share treasures from our own relationship with God — not just recite facts we've picked up along the way. We'll be able to authentically invest in the lives of others, creating atmospheres with impact, that produce powerful opportunities for true and lasting transformation.

In Matthew 13:45, Jesus continues with His examples of the Kingdom: "…the Kingdom of heaven is like a merchant seeking beautiful pearls, who, when he had found one pearl of great price, went and sold all that he had and bought it."

The Pearl of Great Price tells of a discovery that, unlike the Hidden Treasure, is not an accident. The discovery is made by a man who knows what he is looking for and has intentionally gone after it. He's a pearl merchant. This means that he has a personal stake in being able to recognize good quality when he sees it and has probably invested significant time learning about priceless pearls. He understands that the treasure of a lifetime won't come to him but will need to be pursued. He delights in the thrill of the hunt. And once he's found this precious pearl, he too sells everything he has to obtain it. Months, weeks, perhaps years of pursuit have led him to what he had previously only imagined, and he's willing to count the cost to make his dream a reality.

It's interesting to also consider what the merchant is in pursuit of. Pearls are not like other precious stones. There is no refining process after they are found that increases their value. They do not need to be cut or polished, as other gems do. Created out of adversity as the oyster covers its sandy irritation with a pearlescent coating, they need only to be discovered and identified. For the merchant, his process is not in refining the pearl once it is found but rather in his journey of perseverance to find it, as he's intentionally cultivated the ability to recognize its value.

For me, the story of the pearl merchant is the flip-side of the story of the treasure hidden in the field. Jesus is showing us the person who is growing in God through the process of study, meditation, and contemplation. They love the scriptures; they savor quality teaching, dialogue, and excellent conferences. However, learning alone isn't enough for them—just as knowing about the perfect pearl didn't satisfy the merchant. They want a real-life, personal encounter with the God they have been thinking deeply about, and they will continue to gladly seek and keep on seeking until they find it.

Sometimes, we experience the richness of revelation suddenly, stumbling into an encounter that we have little understanding of. We're launched into a process of considering carefully what's happened to us, what the revelation means for our relationship with the Lord, and what it signifies about who He's created us to be. At other times, revelation comes as we intentionally look into the mirror of the Word. We think deeply about who God really is in His fullness, and we commit ourselves to continuing in that truth until we have a very personal encounter with that aspect of His nature. When it happens, we will have made the investment to recognize it.

Since both processes are valid entry points to a greater revelation of the nature of God, choosing to use only one method of process will limit our treasure. If we depend only on stumbling across chance deposits or experiences, we will develop a very happenstance, random relationship with God that is not conducive to progressive maturity. If our noses are buried in books all the time or we only explore through our study guides, we might bypass a wonderful face-to-face encounter with the Author and never realize it! Jesus purposefully told us of two ways to discover a great treasure, so it seems wise to invest equally in both.

Happily Pursuing the Treasure Inside

Colossians 3:3 says that our old life is dead and our new one is hidden in with Christ in God. That's the greatest treasure of all…and it's already in us: Christ IN us, the hope of glory (Colossians 1:27). The treasure of our identity and our destiny is waiting to be discovered. At times, we'll stumble upon it; on other occasions, we'll embark on a focused, determined journey to find it.

But the good news is: it's there! Think of it! If someone told you that there were amazing riches somewhere in your own home, searching for them wouldn't be an onerous obligation but rather an exciting adventure. It wouldn't be hard to put down the TV remote or to get up early to start the process of searching. You might even be able to get your teenagers enthused about it!

This is where the "joy" in Joyful Intentionality comes from. Trying-harder-to-do-better-for-God is displaced by a passionate desire to purposefully engage with God, discovering all of who He is and all of who He created us to be. We become confident that the treasure is there to be discovered, and we joyfully do what it takes to find it. This is the key mindset for Joyfully Intentional people. We embrace a lifestyle of development because we want to, not because we have to.

> **Our passion brings focus and fuel for a process of maturity**
> **that bridges the gap from where we are now to the dream God**
> **has waiting for us.**

The mindsets that we're upgrading on this journey are vast and varied. With that in mind, I've chosen to focus on the areas of transformation in my own perceptions that have had the greatest impact on my journey from trying-harder-to-do-better-for-God to a life that is passion-driven, a life lived joyfully "on purpose":

The joy is in the journey, not just the outcome.

Pursue character: Who do I need to become to do this?

The unexpected is to be expected—and embraced. Love the learning.

Collect, value, process, and treasure what God gives you.

Take risks.

Become a champion receiver.

Make powerful choices.

YOUR CHIEF TRAVELING COMPANION

Most importantly, all of this brilliant thinking can only occur in delightful partnership with the Holy Spirit. Of all the treasures I've discovered in this life, the simplicity and joy found in traveling with Him is one of the greatest. He never sighs with frustration, because He is never frustrated. He will sit with me when I don't understand and either kindly tell me again or hug me when it's a matter of comfort rather than comprehension.

He's a creative, patient, wise teacher who loves revealing A-ha! moments and unwrapping them with me. He is the whisperer of secrets (often at the least convenient times; usually, I think, for His own amusement). He is my endless cheerleader who infuses me with His confidence. After all: He's seen the movie of my life, so He's not gripped about the uncertainties of the current scene. I have felt His smile when I feel invisible to everyone else and have been steadied by His hand on my shoulder when I've been tempted to turn and run.

He is, quite simply, my Best Friend.

And on the most precious days, He reads to me from one of our favorite writings, altering the language to personalize it to our relationship, so that I am reminded once again of how much He loves our life together:

Us Two

"Wherever I go, there's always you.
There's always you and Me.
Whatever I do, you want to do.
"Where are you going today?" says you.
"That's very odd, 'cuz I was too."
"Let's go together," says Me to you.
"Let's go together," says you...

"Let's look for dragons," I say to you.
"Yes, let's," says you to Me.
We crossed the river and found a few —
"Yes, those are dragons all right," says you.
"As soon as I saw their tails, I knew.
That's what they are," says you to Me.
"That's what they are," says you.

"Let's frighten the dragons" I say to you.
"Alright" says you to Me.
"I'm not afraid," I say to you
And I hold your hand and we say "Shoo!
Silly old dragons," and off they flew.

"I wasn't afraid," says you to Me.
"I'm never afraid with You."

So wherever I AM, there's always you.
There's always you and Me.
"What would I do?" I say to You,
"If it wasn't for You," and You say "True".
"It isn't much fun for One, but Two,
Can stick together," says You to me.
"That's how it is" says You.

I first read A.A. Milne's original version of that Winnie-the-Pooh poem when I was six years old. Since then, my journey has taken me over many mountains and through some pretty deep valleys. The simplicity of my relationship with God was often obscured by the shadows of rules and limited by the handcuffs of how-to's. And there are days that I still trip over old traditions and race ahead with silly thoughts. But these words have always drawn me back to the grace and peace that is the Holy Spirit's true nature in our friendship. Yes, whatever You're doing, I want to do too. It actually is, and is becoming, that simple.

Joyful Intentionality, at its very core, is a matter of the heart. It is a life that we embark upon because we have such confidence in the love of the One who has gone first. Mindsets are transformed as we learn to perceive with the eyes of our hearts that are enlightened and as truth bubbles up to renew our thinking. The affection of walking hand-in-hand (even when dragons are present) overwhelms us. We no longer believe; we know. He will not, cannot fail.

We don't engage in a process of development with God in order to gain His approval. No, we become active participants in our spiritual growth because we are responding to His kindness and grace. Over the years, I have come to realize that God always begins a process of development in me by allowing me to see what is missing in our relationship. Because He does it with such kindness, I want to intentionally explore the aspect of His nature that will bridge that gap that has become visible to me. But each and every time, the Holy Spirit always establishes the development in such a way that I know the outcome isn't simply a result of my effort to excel, but results because of His power, love, and commitment to my transformation into the image of Christ. He begins the process. I cooperate with it. He already sees it finished and works in me and through me until I can see it, too. These times of development with Him have established in me a new understanding of the One who is the "Author and Finisher" of my faith (Hebrews 12:2).

So, as we explore the concept of a passionate life lived on purpose, be sure to unwrap your discoveries with the One who delights in journeying with you at all times.

Let Him set the pace and choose your upgrades.

Don't be in a hurry. Pause to reflect.

Savor this first reading as an initial exploration.

And, when you're ready, begin to ponder the questions that will be asked throughout the book and explore with the tools that you'll find at the end. Make it a Divine conversation. Remember, God is not lecturing. Any notes that you might take aren't for a quiz but are a record of your journey together with Him. This isn't an assignment to be completed or a job that needs to be done. It is a path of exploration…and this brings us to our first mindset.

PART 1

Key Mindsets of Joyfully Intentional People

MINDSET #1:
THE JOY OF THE JOURNEY

If you've ever taken an extended road trip, you've probably heard the words, "Are we there yet?" Of the many, *many* times I've heard this phrase, my favorite remains "The Driveway Incident." My car full of kindergartners, I was setting out on a class field trip that required a two-hour drive to the city. We had barely exited the parking lot of the school (and had yet to actually get to the street itself) when the question rang out: "Are we there yet?"

Yes, it was a long day. It always is when the focus of the trip is only on the outcome.

In the Parable of the Talents (Matthew 25) we read, "Well done, good and faithful servant." This phrase tells us that finishing isn't the only goal; instead, it is how we finish and who we've become along the way that is important. We call the time we spend on earth a lifetime for a reason: it takes time to live. If our only focus is getting to the end of a circumstance or season of our lives, then we can easily miss the treasure to be discovered along the way—one that we'll need in order to thrive and finish well—not just survive to the end. Joyfully Intentional people have embraced the joy of the journey, not just arriving at the destination, and that joy continually transforms how we think about life, about God and about the circumstances we encounter on the way.

RUN YOUR OWN RACE

Long distance runners race for a variety of reasons. Speed and time to the finish line are not their only measures. Many will never match a world-class pace, but all have their own uniquely wonderful course to complete. Dick Hoyt is just such a runner. When his teenage son, Rick, came to him and expressed his desire to participate in a 5k fund-raiser for a local boy who had been paralyzed, Dick said "Okay". They ran their first race together and Rick loved it. (Dick says he was just glad he survived it.) Then Rick asked if they could do another race, a marathon. The marathon took more training, but together, they did it. Eventually, they entered the Iron Man Triathlon, one of the most grueling swim/bike/run events on the planet. And together, Dick and Rick finished that one too. Their times were not record setting or even competitive, but everyone was amazed at this father and son running team. You see, Rick was born with cerebral palsy and is a spastic quadriplegic Since 1977, when Rick was fifteen years old, Dick has invented ways to swim, bike and run with his son in tow for over thirty-seven years.

Everyone's race is different and has its own distinctive value. There is no standard in the Kingdom that measures our achievements in quantifiable statistics. The value of our lives will never be in how many books we've read (or written), the years we spent in school, the number of hours that we prayed or how fast we read our Bibles. The standards for success that tend to impress human beings are rarely ones that God shares.

Comparison thinking is a thief, assigned to rob us of the joy of the journey. Focus on God's delight in the exceptional champion He created you to be, running the unique course He has crafted just for you.

The joy of the journey explodes in us when we surrender the lies that are designed to steal it. Imagine getting rid of the weight of these ridiculous comparisons that God isn't making:

"Everyone else seems to be getting it faster than me."

"My friend just had a great breakthrough. Why hasn't mine come?"

"If I had the advantages in life that he's had, I would be able to do that too."

"How will I ever be able to catch to her? She has so much more experience than me."

These are imaginations that Joyfully Intentional people learn to throw down, lock up, and walk over (2 Corinthians 10:5). They think about their thinking and ask: "Who wins with this mindset?"

Look again at the thoughts listed above. Would any of them bring you peace that passes understanding or joy unspeakable and full of glory? Do they sound gentle or kind? People often ask me, "How do I know if it's God or not?" God's voice and His thoughts are filled with the Fruit of the Spirit. They will be patient, kind, merciful, gracious, good, and loving — leaving you with peace and joy. But the fruit of comparison is shame, guilt and insignificance. Comparison doesn't encourage us. It disheartens us in order to keep us from continuing in our race. Satan's only real hope of defeating you is to find ways to get you to compare yourself to others and come up short.

**God is the author of "en-courage-ment" on your journey.
Satan is the author of "dis-courage-ment."
All of us will run our race with "courage,"
but which type of "courage" will we choose?**

Remember the scenes from the movie "Chariots of Fire," where Abrams loses several races at the finish line because he looks to see how his competitor is doing? The need to compare his progress to another runner costs him the victory. That knowledge didn't help him win. In fact, it hindered him. Then consider Eric Liddell, who ran with abandon in a style that was completely unique, but was authentic to him. He ran his own race, his own way, including being true to the values that he believed in. And in the end, Liddell won (in more ways than just receiving an Olympic medal).

The enemy has to convince you to give up because he knows that God has a brilliant race strategy that will not fail. "… let us run with endurance the race that is set before us, looking unto Jesus, the author and finisher of our faith" (Hebrews 12:1b-2a). We find encouragement to finish our journey well by remaining mindful that Jesus ran this course first, and by focusing our vision only on Him. He pioneered this path and promises that Christ in us will gloriously complete it. Our job is to run in stride only with Him and "press towards the goal for the prize of the upward call of God in Christ Jesus" (Philippians 3:14).

Psalm 139:16 says that all your days were written in God's book of your life before you were ever born. That's YOUR book, not someone else's. God has already authored your story from beginning to end and knows the good outcome He intends. Your role is to partner with the Holy Spirit as He reveals your story and leave everyone else to do the same with theirs.

Comparisons that make us feel inferior, or give us a false sense of superiority at someone else's expense, are never from God. Let Him set your pace and course; then run your own race in a state of encouragement knowing that as you follow Him, you'll be right on time for everything He has prepared for you. Dick Hoyt never once acquired a record-setting time in any race he ever ran, and his son, Rick, technically never ran at all! But what they achieved together is inspiring, lasting and powerful. Find the joy in the unique nature of the journey God has created for you.

EFFORT DOESN'T EQUAL DISTANCE COVERED

During my days as an elementary school teacher, I had an unexpected revelation while cleaning the cage of our classroom pet. He was a cute, chubby little hamster and was full of passion, totally committed to running with all his might for hours upon hours—except that his race wasn't on a course that covered distance. His was on a wheel....

A wheel that took him nowhere.

Our hamster never actually went anywhere, but I'm fairly certain that he ran thousands of miles. And that day as I cleaned his cage, it hit me: just the action of running (even with great effort) isn't synonymous with making progress. We can expend huge amounts of energy worrying, replaying old mistakes, figuring out what we need to say or do if this or that happens, or creating ten contingency plans for numerous disasters, but it won't take us anywhere—and it certainly doesn't create joy. It is, however, guaranteed to be totally exhausting.

Just as I had learned that the volume of resources consumed didn't equal maturity, my little hamster exemplified the truth that "energy expended does not equal distance-in-the-Spirit covered."

That day in the classroom, the concept of joy from rest began to open up to me. Rest and peace in Christ is not about how much you are or are not doing. Nor is it about how much sleep you get or how busy your schedule is. Those things can cause your body to be tired (which is a legitimate part of life at times), but true rest is an internal state; it's the consistent inner calm that a world-class runner experiences whether he is battling an uphill climb on the course or sprinting on a downhill section, because he knows that every step is taking him closer to his finish line.

Rest comes from knowing that you're covering ground on the race course that God has uniquely designed for you. No matter what is occurring, you are partnering with Him to use it to grow stronger, rest deeper and rise higher, taking both internal and external territory as you go. It may not always be easy, but you experience a sense of ease as He sets the pace.

People who try to find rest by getting to the end of all their checklists or by totaling up their tasks that have been accomplished will never find it. Their wheel of endless jobs to be done will just circle around again and again. Their never ending sense of "If only I can just…" repeats over and over and over. Exhausted from believing that peace is achieved by getting everything finished, they pause momentarily on their wheel of performance. But soon, like the hamster, they're running again, with their heads tucked down and little legs churning faster—hoping that *this* time, with a little more effort, they will make some progress towards the joy of the journey that seems so elusive.

That day in my classroom, as I watched the hopeful little hamster racing in circles on his wheel towards a nonexistent finish line, I realized that I had a lot in common with him. I'd been racing on my own wheel for years, not understanding that a "checklist life" with God was not the life that He wanted for me. He had prepared an adventure—a life to be explored without limits in a wide-open territory. But the enemy had substituted adventure and exploration with a performance wheel to nowhere, in hopes that I would never learn the difference.

However, when I began to see God as He really is (kind, good, gentle, faithful, loving and full of joy and delight in who He made me to be), we began to run and explore together. I traded the frustration of an endless, predictable wheel to nowhere for the joy of an often unpredictable but encouraging journey that's always going somewhere.

EMBRACE ADVERSITY

Often, the very elements that can accelerate our process the most are the very situations that we try our hardest to avoid. When obstacles appear on our horizon, we are prone to view them as negatives. Whether the obstacle is an authentic attack of the enemy that is meant to delay or deter us, or it's an opportunity for transformation that God has wisely allowed, we must look at it through the lens of grace. Otherwise, we may miss seeing Holy Spirit as our Comforter (or the faithful Father, or Jesus as our Friend) who is holding out His hand to us in an invitation to get to know a new aspect of His true nature that we've never seen before.

Adversity and acceleration are partners on this journey; they work as a team. In the Bible, Joshua's leadership was established in Israel with what seemed to be an insane battle plan to take a massive, fortified city by silently marching around its walls until it was time to shout. David accelerated from being a shepherd boy to a national hero after defeating a very large giant who had paralyzed an entire army. An outbreak of persecution forced the early Church out of the comfort zone of Jerusalem, allowing them new opportunities to share the Gospel throughout a much greater territory. Daniel gained favor and influence with kings while petting hungry lions on the head.

Tough times, challenges and obstacles that the enemy has designed to take us out of the race can be the very occasions that God smiles at, knowing who He plans to be for us as we encounter Him in a new way. Nothing infuriates our adversary more than having the very thing that was meant to discourage us become an opportunity for acceleration, advancement and upgrade. He continually seems to forget that we don't need to know God as the Faithful One when we're surrounded by loyal friends. Encountering the Holy Spirit as Teacher isn't so necessary when we've got life all figured out. A happy heart doesn't need a Comforter, but a broken one does. When we can change, "Why do these things always happen to me?" and choose instead to focus on Who God will be for us now in this unique place — we deal the devil a staggering blow and commit a fabulous act of war. We've turned the obstacle meant to destroy us into an opportunity to become stronger in Christ.

During my years in education, I had a colleague who was a long-distance runner. His dream was to run the Boston Marathon; but in order to do that, he needed a certain qualifying time in another race. As his preliminary race, he chose the Big Sur Marathon, a course that runners consider to be one of the hardest in the country because of its countless steep hills and tough terrain. Big Sur had to be one of the most absurd choices my friend could have made to obtain the race time that he needed to qualify for Boston.

When I asked him why he chose Big Sur as his qualifier, his answer was quite direct. "Because Boston is famous for 'Heartbreak Hill'. I want to have run a race with ten hills tougher than 'Heartbreak' so that when I get to that point in Boston, I'll know that I can do it...and more." Smart man. He wasn't just trying to survive a race. He was choosing to transform his identity as a runner to being a "runner of impossible hills."

**He had decided to use the obstacles of today
to fuel the opportunities of tomorrow.**

Joyfully Intentional people know the value of adversity on their journey, and they train for it. For them, it is not something to be avoided, but to be expected. One of the Bible promises that no one ever puts on a pretty refrigerator magnet is: "In this world, you will have tribulation." No "maybe" or "you might encounter." Nope. It's going be there, so prepare yourself. Jesus told His disciples just how to prepare — and it wasn't with cynicism that expects the worst. "Cheer up!" was the key He gave them and us. "I've overcome the world" (John 16:33).

That wisdom increases in its impact when we consider that He shared it as He was preparing to face the cross just a few hours later — the greatest adversity of all. It was such a statement of confidence in His Father, since Jesus hadn't actually walked out all the steps of overcoming the world yet. He faced a pretty rough night ahead: betrayal, isolation, beatings, the crushing weight of sin, separation from His Father, and a tortuous death. Yet, Jesus already saw Himself as an overcomer. The shame of the world's iniquity was awful for Him. He despised it, but He endured it by purposely connecting with the joy ahead (Hebrews 12:2).

Now *that's* Joyful Intentionality.

In essence, Jesus had trained all of His earthly life for that moment in time—by growing in grace with God, through developing a deep relationship with His Father, and by gaining experience in overcoming temptation and tribulation many different ways. When that night of His greatest adversity began, John 13 says that Jesus *knew* that the Father had now given all things into His hands and that He *knew* that He had come from God and was going to God. Everything He had gone through before that night (both the triumphs and the challenges) had created in Him a deep, unshakable knowledge of who His Father was to Him and all that He had been born to be. He *knew* the eternal outcome that was possible, and that outcome was the joy that He focused on. It would literally carry Him to hell and back.

There is a Navy Seal motto that says: "In the heat of battle, you will not rise to the occasion, but will revert to the level of your training." To finish our race well with joy, we will need to embrace our challenges as opportunities that will strengthen us to make it to the end—no matter how many "Heartbreak Hills" we encounter. We purposely practice by rejoicing always and giving thanks in everything (1 Thessalonians 5:18), knowing that the obstacles of today are our practice grounds for finishing well tomorrow.

THE RELATIONSHIP IS THE JOURNEY

Our "journey" is not what we achieve in ministry or a long list of our accomplishments. It isn't based on the people we've met or where we've traveled. Discovering God Himself is the journey, and our relationship with Him is the course we run. When Jesus spoke about the eternal finish line at the end of the age in Matthew 7:23, it isn't the miracles or deliverances that will matter in the end, but it will be whether or not we are intimately known by Him. As He closes the doors of Heaven, He won't say "You didn't work hard enough" or "You should have done something more spectacular". Instead, He will say, "You need to leave now. I don't know who you are. We never had a deeply personal relationship" (my version of Matthew 7:23).

Each of us wants to impact our world, our communities, our families and those we love. But all we can ever give away in ministry is our own relationship with God. "When they saw the courage of Peter and John and realized that they were unschooled, ordinary men, they were astonished and they took note: These men had been with Jesus" (Acts 4:13).

Joyfully Intentional people know that relationship with God IS the journey, and knowing Him in it is the greatest joy of all.

Paul described it in one of my most beloved scriptures in all of the Bible. If there is one ambition in my life, these words capture it completely,

"For my *determined* purpose is that I may know Him; that I may become more progressively and deeply acquainted with Him, perceiving and recognizing and understanding the wonders of His person...."
(Philippians 3:10, Amplified Bible *italics mine*)

This verse is the very essence of a passion driven life that's lived with determined purpose. It's the progressive path of knowing God in all His manifestations. It's knowing Him as Father and everything that comes with His Fatherhood. It's knowing Jesus as Savior, as Lord, as the Friend who sticks closer than a brother, as Wonderful Counselor and as King of Kings. It's our intimate friendship with the Holy Spirit as Comforter, genius Teacher and steadfast Helper...just to name a few of the "wonders of His person." It's perceiving who He wants to be for us in any circumstance, recognizing Him and knowing how He thinks and loves. It is living in the understanding and wisdom of His grace, mercy, love, kindness...and it goes on and on. One life is really far too short a time to truly explore His wonders. Thank God for eternity.

The guys at the end of the age that Jesus talked about in Luke 16 had confused "knowing about" Him with "knowing and being known." Their idea of relationship is like someone who mistakes their supermarket tabloid knowledge of a celebrity for an actual friendship. You might buy and read every magazine that's ever printed a story about your favorite movie star, but it doesn't mean that you are their friend. If you met them on the street, you might be able to tell them all about their lives: the names of their children, their favorite food and where they like to vacation. *But they wouldn't know you.* They've never met you. You are a stranger to them.

I had a supermarket tabloid relationship with God for years, reducing Him to human proportions that I could quantify and understand. There were bread crumbs of authenticity in our relationship, but they were eclipsed by my insecure need for achievement as proof of my value. I was proud of how much I knew about Jesus; I even had a degree in Bible to prove it. Yet I was clueless. I didn't really know who He was.

But my tabloid relationship with Him changed one night in 1995. I had received prayer in a ministry line and was sitting on the ground as the rest of the people around me were being prayed for. Suddenly, there was Jesus, standing right in front of me. His presence was so overwhelming that I couldn't look up. Everything seemed impossibly bright, and the love I felt radiating from Him invaded every cell in my body until it hummed with joy, delight, and peace.

Such tangible love provoked an immediate, passionate response within me. All I wanted was to do was give Him something. So I reached inside my chest (which I could apparently do since we were no longer dealing in an earthbound realm) because I wanted to give Him my heart. I guess I thought that I would pull out this lovely, Valentine's Day looking object — but instead, my hand was filled with filth. Not just dirt…*filth*, so vile that it was actually moving.

There are no words for the embarrassment I felt; I can only describe it as absolute horror. I panicked. I desperately reached back inside my chest, attempting to find the real heart that obviously I had missed. Yet when I pulled my hand out again, the same putrid rot was there. And instead of stopping, I just kept repeating this action over and over — until there was a mound of squirming filth about two feet high all over the feet of Jesus.

I was exhausted. I was empty. I wanted to die. Here was Jesus, whom I adored and this was the best I had to give Him. Why was I even alive?

And then He did something that changed everything.

In the kindest voice I've ever heard, He simply said, "I'll take it." And He did. He picked it all up, pressed it to His chest, and it disappeared. No shame. Without cringing or disgust, He took it all.

I've never recovered from that moment. Thankfully, I know now that I never will. I still don't understand the depths of all that happened that night, and for many years I didn't even try to understand. But I became a different person because of that encounter, though I didn't magically transform overnight in my thinking, language and behavior. That continues to be an on-going process. But I beheld the Philippians 3:10 "wonders of His person" in a way that imparted a glimpse of Who He really is that continues to captivate me.

In recent years, I've entered into a new conversation with God about what happened to me that night on the floor in front of Jesus. What was it that I pulled out of me?

After a great deal of pondering and listening, I've come to understand much more than I did before. I know now that the filth I pulled out of myself was my "Old Man," the one who is dead (Colossians 3:3). My life was now hidden with God, in Christ. I didn't have to be transporting my Old Man around anymore, but I was. And like any dead thing in the natural, it had rotted. My religious ideas about a legalistic God left me continually trying to dress up my old self to be acceptable to Him. It was a hopeless cause that had left me exhausted and ashamed. There's no makeover for a rotting corpse; yet that's just what I had tried to do with all my self-improvement efforts. On that evening in 1995, my moment had come to truly "reckon myself dead to sin, but alive to God in Christ Jesus" (Romans 6:11). I could keep trying-harder-to-do-better to fix up this "old Allison," but it wasn't going to work. She was dead already… and God found a creative way of showing me just how dead she really was. And the reason it disappeared in His hands? Because He had already taken all that sin away 2,000 years ago. I was the only one that could see it. For Him, it had been buried long ago in the deepest sea.

Instead, it was time to embark on a journey of discovery of Christ in me, my hope of glory; of who He really is and who I really am in Him.

I don't consider that night to be a "supernatural" encounter as much as I see it as God naturally being Himself in my world. It certainly doesn't make my journey more significant than anyone else's, and I can't say that it has made my process easier either (which I always imagined such an experience would)—just different. If anything, I think it occurred because

11

I had been rather thick-headed and hard-hearted. God had been trying to have that conversation with me for years, but I didn't have ears to hear. They were plugged-up with the checklists and self-improvement inventories that I adored. So He graciously invaded my warped world instead — knowing it would take years for me to unwrap what He imparted, and He was kindly hoping that we could get on with that.

Most people are much brighter and are more sensitive to the Spirit of God than I was. With them, He has been able to speak in whispers, nods, and nudges. If that's your story, good for you. Thanks for extending grace to those of us who are more like Paul on the Damascus road; who have become so blind that we've needed some direct, Divine intervention to get us back on the relational journey that God treasures most.

That's why there's such joy in this great road trip of life, because God has so much delight in it! God initiated a relationship with people out of His passionate desire for friends. He saw no fun in creating a people who just passively ride through life on a motorized airport walkway to our final destination. He's a good Father, whose greatest pleasure is feeling our trusting hand in His as we say, "Where to now, Papa?" It's *being* with us that He adores.

In journeying with Him, life ceases to be only about getting to an outcome. We even find ourselves glad when our path ends up being a little longer than we anticipated or takes an unexpected curve. Rather than a disappointment or delay, it's simply more time to travel with and be loved by Him. And we revel in the peace, renewal, and encouragement found in the joy of the journey.

Mindset #1: The Joy of the Journey

1. What parts of your current journey are you really enjoying?

2. What is an area of adversity that you're realizing is a great place to practice your learning?

3. Who does God want to show up as in this situation?

4. What is your partnership with Him developing in you?

5. Which have you been considering more: the journey of development or just trying to survive to get to the outcome? Is there an upgrade in your perspective in this? What is it?

6. Go back to question #1. Is there something in what you're enjoying in the journey that could encourage you in overcoming your adversities? Ask the Holy Spirit how to use these to encourage yourself in Him. Take notes about what you discover together.

MINDSET #2:
WHO DO I WANT TO BECOME?

For years, I seemed surrounded by friends who all had multiple and very specific prophetic words about their lives. They knew what countries they were called to, what kind of work they were meant to do, and what their job description in the Kingdom was.

Me? I didn't have anything like that. I only had two prophetic words, and only one of them contained any detailed information: "You will have a significant voice within the ministry that you're currently connected to." And when God lifted me out of that ministry in a Divine "suddenly" moment, it appeared that even my one specific word had evaporated.

I eventually had the opportunity to receive more prophetic ministry at a series of conferences I attended, but the words weren't at all what I was hoping for. They gave me no useful details whatsoever about what I was going to do in my life.

Instead, every single word was about character.

While people all around me were getting outrageously life-specific information, I was told:

"You constantly seek Him with a Divine 'Yes!' on your lips."

"You are a woman of significant faith."

"You create an atmosphere where people connect with who God really is because of the authenticity of who you are."

"You lean towards majesty."

"You live to fight. You love the fight. You are an exquisite warrior who can endure."

Yes, those are all great words. All very affirming. But I foolishly wanted *details*. What will I be doing? Where will I do it? When? How? In the months that followed, God graciously let me chase my tail about the details while He continued to pile on the "character" words — probably for His own amusement.

BE CAREFUL WHAT YOU WISH FOR

Eventually, a quite necessary process of maturity began for me as I watched events unfold in the life of an acquaintance who'd received a very specific word about his life from a reliable, proven prophetic minister — the kind of word I had longed for. It described his ministry in detail. It said who he would be connected with and described what would be involved.

But over time, I began to realize that this person filtered everything through that word. Potential events or personal contacts were always evaluated from a mindset of, "Is this a place or someone that is part of my word coming to pass?" He speculated extensively as to what, when, and how his destiny would reveal itself. I watched as he missed key opportunities because they didn't seem to fit with the details of his word. When events didn't happen as he imagined, offense and disillusionment gained ground in his thinking. Now (though God is well able to redeem this season of his life) he is no longer actively pursuing this part of his journey.

Watching his choices provided a profound learning opportunity for me. As I began to see how much of a performance addict my unredeemed self had been, I realized that my lack of life-specific prophetic words was actually a merciful gift. The Father had graciously focused on telling me who I would become in character and persona, rather than what I would be doing or who I would be doing it with. It allowed me to focus on my identity in Him rather than details to figure out. He wasn't being difficult. He was being kind. It was the beginning of another mindset shift.

**Focus on maturing into who you are becoming,
and leave the details of how, when, and where in God's hands.**

My questions became about identity: who God really is and who He made me to really be. Every situation I encountered was embraced as training for reigning, not evaluated as relevant or irrelevant to a specific destiny.

COOPERATING WITH THE PROCESS

For my unique journey, my role was to cooperate with any process that God initiated — even if I didn't understand what it was for at the time. We went through periods in which worship was the focus of His process, and I built up stamina in praise. Part of my development for a year was to make a 400 mile round trip once a month to participate in a worship evening called "Sacred Space" — an hour and a half of ministering to the Lord. No teaching. No praying. Just worship. And even though many of the people I worshipped with would later become great friends, I never spoke to anyone. I never actively sought to make any connections, because at the time, I didn't know there was anyone or anything besides God to connect with. I only knew that God had said to come there to worship. And while those evenings were truly times of Heaven on earth, it was not only the time that I spent in the sanctuary but also the hours that I spent driving to and from the location that were transformational. I had some of the most delightful, intimate conversations with God during those trips, and the mysteries He shared then remain priceless gifts that I am still unwrapping today.

Long before I ever considered the prophetic as a significant part of my calling, God initiated having me write out prophetic words of encouragement for friends or from His heart to mine. Often it would seem that the words were for no one in particular; but then He'd point someone out to me and say, "That one is for them." A few years later, His focus was on learning how to talk to Him for hours in prayer, usually as I was walking, driving or hiking. I discovered that intercession didn't always have to take place in a "prayer closet" and that I had a lot of rules about prayer that God didn't have. Many of the mindsets about intercession that we are upgrading in The Warrior Class come from those days, though at the time, I couldn't have conceived of leading a community of intercessors because I didn't know that I was one!

What was happening during those times that didn't seem to connect to any specific purpose in my life? I was building a deeper relationship with God — which is the greatest purpose of all. I was learning to respond to what He initiated. I gained sensitivity to His promptings and had opportunities to endure in prolonged adversities, to learn that He can always be trusted.

Even in the areas of my life in which I was actively involved in ministry, I was being trained for a future I didn't comprehend. I spent fifteen years serving with a precious group of women in Aglow Prison Ministry, sharing God's love in two of the largest women's prisons in the U.S. at that time. We experienced amazing encounters with God during those years: phenomenal life transformations, miracles of healing, outrageous grace. In prison, I learned the *power* of love and the simplicity of the Gospel. When I accepted the job of developing leaders for that ministry, I learned how to write training guides and how to mentor people towards their full potential. And every week, I practiced speaking publicly to an audience that ranged from wildly supportive to openly hostile. It taught me to focus on my audience of One, no matter what was occurring around me.

All of these times of learning and process have impacted who I am and what I do today — though only a few years ago, I could never have imagined my life as it is now. I received no clear prophetic words about my current ministry, but God has perfectly prepared me for it. My greatest role in my journey was to continually say "Yes" and take risks — not because I always understood what it was for, but because God opened a door of opportunity. Some risks were grand successes. Others? Not so much! But all of them contributed to my ongoing process of maturity that continues today.

As He takes us through process, God not only walks with us so that we can learn that He can be trusted, but also so He can discover how much we can be entrusted with. Not because we are earning a promotion, but because He is wise enough to know the spiritual muscle and sensitivity we will need to thrive at the next level of the Kingdom, instead of being overwhelmed by it. Is our faithfulness situational? Is it founded on His nature, or on our circumstances? Is our obedience based in love and relationship with Him, or is it rooted in a fear of His disapproval? Will we cling to the ownership of our money, time, and reputation—or have we learned that we are simply stewards of our lives? A good steward can be entrusted with a great deal, because they know how to invest for the joy of bringing a good return to their Master (Matthew 25:20-21).

And when God allows refining circumstances in our process, it is because He is kindly training us for what we'll be carrying as part of our destiny. Often, what we interpret as delays and lack of clarity is His way of sharpening our focus or of showing us gaps in our lives that He has plans to fill with who He wants to be for us instead. In His kindness, He foresees where we are needlessly vulnerable and desires to equip us for what He knows is ahead.

Fulfilling our Kingdom destiny is not about being worthy.
It's about preparation that aligns us with the One who is.

Our character is meant to grow up alongside our gifting and destiny in the Kingdom. One does not precede the other. Gifts and anointing are not rewards for good behavior. They are given by God unconditionally (Romans 11:29), and He excels in crafting a process of development for us so that we learn to thrive in who we are as we walk in what we were created to do. We invest in our development because we've become so very captivated by growing up into all things in Christ (Ephesians 4:15)—not because we're trying harder to be better suited for a particular destiny. The burden is never on us to be ready. Our role is simply to recognize and intentionally cooperate with the process of maturity that God initiates. If we do that, we'll be perfectly prepared and aligned with Him when the details finally become clear.

THE VALUE OF PREPARATION

It's like the Parable of the Ten Virgins (Matthew 25): all ten arrived at the wedding celebration with lamps in hand, but while five virgins brought lamps that were already filled, the other five came with empty vessels. From outward appearances, you wouldn't have been able to tell the difference. The difference only became apparent when they were awakened suddenly by the door to the feast being thrown open and the invitation came to join the Bridegroom. The ones without oil were not ready. They tried to get the others who came prepared to share with them, but it was too late.

In this story, I see God's unique pattern for our preparation in life. I've rarely known in advance when or where His entry to opportunity will open, but I'm passionate about being ready when it does. Working from the premise that *everything* is useful for development, my first question to God in every situation has become, "What part of my true identity and our relationship are You developing now?" — not, "What is this for?"

Life isn't "All of God; none of me." That may sound humble, but it's a very human version of humility, one that God doesn't have. "All of Him" opens up the doors to our next celebration of the Kingdom as His beloved one, but "*all* of me" needs to be prepared for those doors to open: *full* of the oil of our relationship with the Holy Spirit, ready to bring our light into the room — a contribution that brightens up the place! When fullness is the life that we live continually, we can be at rest and at peace as we wait for the door to open. We're content to wait as long as needed, knowing that we've invested wisely and can trust that His preparation will be exactly what we need when we need it.

And there's a difference between the rest that comes from being prepared and passivity that depends on others to build our relationship with God for us. The virgins with full lamps were at rest because they knew they were ready. The virgins with the empty lamps were unprepared due to passivity. When the opportunity came to join the Bridegroom at the feast, everyone was expected to be prepared, to have their own oil. Like the virgins, when our door of opportunity opens, we can't expect to borrow any lacking spiritual maturity from the spiritually mature people we've been hanging out with. There's a personal, relational process with God that we *all* need to engage in. According to this parable, asking others for what they've cultivated in relationship with the Spirit — instead of intentionally developing your own relationship — is not allowed in the Kingdom.

How kind of God to show us that even the processes we don't always understand are essential, and their benefit will be obvious when it's time to move forward. When we can't figure out how our present circumstances are helpful to our development, it's encouraging to know that it's another day to fill my lamp. We can ask the Holy Spirit for enlightenment, but He may or may not answer, depending on what He's building in us. He may ask you to trust His higher ways, to simply know that together with Him, you will be ready when the door opens for you. Knowing that truth brings joy to any circumstance. We trust that our process is presently increasing our love, faith, trust, patience, gentleness, perseverance, or likeness to the image of Christ.

EMBRACE YOUR UNIQUE EXPERIENCE

Not everyone's experience is like mine. Maybe you're someone who *does* have very specific promises or prophetic words. If you do, that's great! It's another authentic path to becoming everything He created you to be. Celebrate them while you're partnering with the Holy Spirit to discover His process of development for you, so that you become all that He has promised.

But if you're like I was—and you don't have lots of details—don't be discouraged by the stories of others who have those types of words. God doesn't work with the same type of prophetic economy that people are prone to. He doesn't classify words as *better* or *less*. If it's truly the Word of the Lord for you, then it's always His very best, given with His whole heart. And *both* types of words will require a Joyfully Intentional process of development.

One of my closest friends received very specific words—about what country he would live in, what he would do there, and what his role in the Kingdom would be. By his own account, the gap between those words and who he was when they were given to him was so huge that it was evident that it would indeed take God to fulfill them. But he had good mentors who taught him that personal prophecy is not magic. It is not inevitable, but contains the *potential* God has for us. Prophecy is often given to us so that when we encounter obstacles, we can overcome them through our faith in the word of the Lord to us (1 Timothy 1:18). They also give us a compass for our development and offer an encouraging glimpse at the good outcome intended by the Lord.

With that in mind, my friend put his hand fearlessly into the hand of the Holy Spirit and pursued a path of development that was intentional, joyful, and focused. He looked at his promises and prophecies, and he painted for himself an accurate inner picture about what kind of character it would require to successfully live in those words. Then, he purposefully began to partner with God in the process needed to develop that character and took practical steps of training and faith. Many of his prophetic words have come to pass, but very few happened the way he thought they would. I've seen my friend's wisdom to leave room for God to take care of the how, when, and where, even when he seems to have a number of details. He still has words that he hasn't seen the fullness of yet, and it remains highly instructive for me to watch him continue to cooperate with God in the relational development of both the skills and the character that those words will require.

DESTINY CAN BE PRACTICAL

Cultivating who we are can be practical as well as spiritual. I have friends who received prophetic words about being a writer, so they took writing classes. Others have promises about particular places they will influence, so they've traveled there to explore the landscape. Often, it required faith to finance their trips, but that became part of their learning process as well!

I have words about my "brilliant voice." While public speaking is something I've done for a while, I continually work on improving my verbal communication. I'm an extrovert with lots of words (which can be helpful at times, and not so much at others). I can be very animated when I speak, but being concise is also a necessary skill. So, I regularly participate in one of the most uncomfortable forms of development that I've discovered so far: I listen to recordings of my talks.

Listening still has a cringe factor for me, but it's easier than it used to be. I have decided to appreciate the continual upgrade in my ability to be targeted with my words, and I also understand that this will be contested territory. The enemy rarely gives up the ground of our promises without a fight. Be aware. He won't just bring others to discourage you, but he'll also work to get you to cooperate with his condemnation.

I was reminded of this recently, when my practice of intentionally listening slipped into bemoaning what I didn't like in my last talk. My brilliant assistant came alongside me to help me realign my thinking. She simply said, "Remember: Satan hates your voice because it does a great deal of damage to the darkness. Let's not agree with him." She was absolutely right. It was fine for me to assess my work so that it would improve, but I needed to do it with the same grace towards myself that God uses in all of His interactions with me.

Practice on purpose. Be realistic in your assessment. But always allocate the same amount of grace towards yourself that God does.

Our willingness to really love the learning, to humble ourselves in training, and to leave our comfort zones are all vital aspects of who we become. As one of my great mentors told me, our dedication to process can be determined simply by asking ourselves one question: "How much do you really want this?" Our development isn't just about the preparation of gifts or skills, but about the necessary peace that we cultivate in knowing we're in the hands of the One who can be trusted as we willingly remain on the Potter's wheel. If we're asking others to submit to the hands of a God who can be depended upon at all times, then we can expect occasions where we must voluntarily do the same.

Remember: there is joy to be found in every process, whether we would call it a success or a failure. There's great delight to be had in knowing how excited God is to see us grow in both spiritual and practical ways. He doesn't separate our lives into ministry and everyday living; it's all life in Him! He rejoices over us like a Dad on Christmas morning who is watching His child squeal over the gifts that He's been delighted to give—deeply satisfied to watch us unwrap them, experiment with them, and explore how they work. He loves it when we come to Him to ask for help in learning how to use them, to soak in the relationship of sitting side-by-side to play or build together. We bring Him happiness when we continue to grow, discovering a new relationship with Him at every stage of our development. He smiles to see Himself reflected in our thoughts and actions. "That's my girl!" He says, or "Look at my son!"

Whether you have details about your life or don't, in either case the focus of those who consistently walk into their destiny is always on who they will need to be, not only on what they will do. We value our promises, treasure what the Lord has said to us, and actively participate in our development. We're not conspiring to make something happen; we're working out our salvation (Philippians 2:12). We choose to see every situation "The Good, The Bad, and The Ugly" (which is my cell phone ringtone, just to remind me...) as an opportunity to grow into the character needed so that when the day comes for us to step into another piece of our Divine destiny, we will be like the virgins whose lamps were full of oil: ready to cross the threshold into our next great adventure.

Mindset #2: Who Do You Want To Become?

1. What key strengths or positive character attributes would you use to describe yourself currently? (List three to five.)

- Sojourner   - advocate for others
- passion
- deep
- compassionate

2. What are your three to five greatest character challenges?

- loving/advocating for myself
- trigger/thinking   - perfectionism/performance
- not flaws → challenges   - defensive
  - living in the past

3. Describe your character if you were living in the fullness of your promises, scriptures and/or prophetic words.

I would live into Joshua 1 and Kingdom living

4. What are the character gaps between who you are now and who you feel destined to be?

- learn to set boundaries
- enjoy learning
- need to receive/have grace for myself

5. Are there circumstances currently in your life that are helping you develop in any of these areas? What do you think they are working in you?

MINDSET #3:
THE UNEXPECTED IS TO BE EXPECTED

Some of my favorite day trips are the ones that are not planned—mornings where my husband Randy and I just jump in our car and decide to go somewhere. We pick a direction and then we're off to see what we can discover. On one of our recent adventures, we found ourselves surrounded by a herd of weed-eating goats, met a turkey who (like a dog) would come to you on command, zip-lined over tree tops, and went rappelling in a cave! Sometimes we'll end up at the movies. Once, we almost got stuck on the back road of a random mountain pass. Fortunately, that turned out to be a "We almost..." story rather than "Remember when the tow truck barely got there before dark?" No matter what the outcome, we both enjoy our days of exploration, of not knowing what's going to happen next.

At other times, we investigate possible destinations for our trips, research what is in the area that might interest us and read reviews from others who have been to that region. We weigh the distance, costs and possibilities for a weekend or a week away that we will both enjoy. While we make basic arrangements, we don't usually have a day-to-day schedule. Our style is to go and begin to check things out from the list of options that we've read about, then decide each day what to do based on weather and what we want to see.

Both of these are authentic ways to travel: one is spontaneous, the other involves more planning, however in each case, there is an element of flexibility that allows for the unexpected. Unforeseen circumstances are not an obstacle, but opportunities that we anticipate and allow room for.

With Joyful Intentionality, while we are purposeful in preparation, we actively anticipate that the Lord will direct our steps in ways we can't possibly imagine. "A man's heart plans his way, but the Lord directs his steps" (Proverbs 16:9). It's a both/and statement, not an either/or one. When we live as beloved ones, we want to go in the direction that God is going. With a sense of His permission, we are free to make plans, working from the premise that, to the best of our understanding, we are following His way for us. But when it's time to step out, we choose to hold the Father's hand rather than clutch tightly to our preconceptions. We live fully aware that His ways have priority over our plans.

Joyfully Intentional people anticipate that life will not unfold as we expect it to, because that would incredibly boring! We rarely know where our path will deviate from what we've planned, but we look forward to finding out — because it's the twists and turns of life that hold some of our best opportunities for laughter and learning. These unexpected events are times where our faith and trust grows in the unchangeable nature of Who we're following, and we become willing to exchange our map for a compass and His kiss. It's when we can let go of details, embracing instead the True North of Who God is at all times and His loving permission to explore His endless possibilities. We can rest in full assurance that, if we get lost, He will find us; but, in the meantime, we're likely to discover something wonderful along roads less travelled.

PROMISES OR DETAILS?

Surprises are occasions in life that allow us to choose to abandon our false sense of security found in having the perfect plan — to let go of our day dream that if we only knew the how, why, where, and when, we would be at rest. That sense of safety is an illusion, a cheap substitute for the peace that passes understanding. These unexpected events that we often label "tests of faith" are, more often, simply evidence that God was being merciful by not sharing that part of our lives with us in advance. If He told us all the details about every step of our journey all at once, we'd probably never even start!

Imagine if Jesus' first words to Peter ("Come follow Me, and I'll make you a fisher of men." Matthew 4:18) had instead been something like this:

"Hey, Pete! I'm Jesus. We're going to be great friends. You're going to leave your job, your family, and your income to travel with Me. You'll do lots of great miracles, but you're also going to say some really stupid things that come from the mind of Satan himself (Matthew 16:23).

"You'll be the first one of my friends that My Dad tells My true identity to. But, after years of friendship, the day will also come when you will be so scared of getting in trouble with the authorities that you'll tell everyone you don't even know who I am…and I'll hear you say that. Right after I hear you, I'll be killed unjustly in a torturous, bloody way, and the work you've been a vital part of building will seem to completely fall apart. But then I'll come back to life, share some important stuff with you, and then I'll go back to Heaven.

"After that all happens, you'll meet God in a new way as the Holy Spirit, and He will change everything in an event that'll involve a lot of wind and fire. You're going to be a very good preacher with loads of impact, but you'll also spend a lot of time getting beaten up, tortured, and thrown in jail. Angels will help you out on occasion.

"You'll have major arguments with your ministry team about some stuff. Oh, and you're gonna be a writer. What you write will be included in a book that we'll call the Bible. Don't worry about the fact that you don't have an education: the Holy Spirit (Who you don't know yet) will tell you what to say and will help you. And the best part? More than likely, you'll get to die in the same horrible way I will…but upside down…. Okay. Off we go!"

Do you *really* want to know everything that's coming? I don't. I'd much rather choose to know that The One will be with me in the unexpected events in my life and put my faith in my Friend who promises that He:

- Never leaves me, nor forsakes me (Hebrews 13:5)

- Is faithful, even if I am faithless (2 Timothy 2:13)

- Loves me with an everlasting, never changing love (Jeremiah 31:3)

- Doesn't consider me merely a servant, but a friend (John 15:15)

- Gives me rest (Matthew 11:28-29)

- Meets all my needs (Matthew 6:31-33 and Philippians 4:19)

- Gives me a peace that isn't available in the world (John 14:27)

- Teaches me the way to go (Psalm 32:8) and guides me into all truth (John 16:13)

- Always hears me (Isaiah 65:24)

- Shares His wisdom with me without wondering why I don't know it already (James 1:5)

- Keeps me healthy and renews my strength (Isaiah 40:31)

- Strengthens me to do all things (Philippians 4:13)

This list could go on for pages. Hmm...promises or details? I'll take promises!

Joyfully Intentional people make a choice to trust in Who more than what, where, how, or why. God may or may not answer questions we have about details. But He'll always answer when we ask Who He wants to be for us, in us, and through us.

SEEING BIBLE HEROES WITH FRESH EYES

It's important to read the stories in the Bible from the viewpoint of the people who lived them. It's easy to read on the surface, thinking, "Yeah, but it turned out okay for them." We've already seen the flannel board story or the technicolor movie, and we know how their story ends...*but they didn't.* They didn't know the outcome. In story after story, time and again, not only did the unexpected occur, but the ludicrous and absurd! And each individual that we read about had to make their own intentional choice to go forward, trusting God.

Consider Moses: backed up against the Red Sea, a world-class army closing fast, and a million panicked, screaming people blaming him for bringing them into the wilderness to die. Talk about being unappreciated! In the midst of this chaos and calamity, he turns to God for a plan. And God replies with a great piece of specific direction: "Stretch out your rod. I'll part the Red Sea. You'll go across. The Egyptians will follow and I'll drown them all" (Exodus 14:15-18).

Reading on the surface, we instantly imagine the Cecil B. DeMille movie scene that follows (where the waves part and the Israelites dance across), but stop to think about it a little more deeply. Yes, it's a great plan...but picture yourself as the one who just heard it. "How does waving a stick do all of that—part a sea, drown an army? Sure, the stick does some other nifty stuff, like that time it turned into a snake... but that's not really helpful at the moment! Wait—it did turn water into blood...but this is already the Red Sea, right? Those were impressive, but opening up an entire body of water? That's a lot to ask of a stick." I think, standing in Moses' shoes, I would have had more questions.

Of course, in the story of the Burning Bush, Moses did have more questions—lots of them. Most of them began with "What if...?" because the plan that was being outlined had a lot of details that didn't make sense. I think we give Moses a tough time about that conversation. It's easy to be a Monday morning quarterback with Bible stories. We've seen the final score...but those we read about were still in the middle of their game. Choose one of these Bible stories, and read below the surface. Imagine your own modern day scenario of the same story, with yourself as the main character. What would you do?

What would you *really* do?

Moses gives me so much hope. His isn't the story of an instant hero but rather of a willing man. And even though his initial "willingness" isn't particularly stellar, he still obeys. By the time we follow his journey with God to the Red Sea, Moses is demonstrating serious signs of life transformation. He's no longer the beaten down, murderer-in-exile, fearful, insecure shepherd that encountered God at the Burning Bush. When the Lord shares His idea for deliverance at the Red Sea, Moses has heard these kinds of plans before and is experiencing who God will be for him in these places. I'm not sure if he's quite "loving the learning" yet...but he's well on his way, because He does what God says without asking further questions. Whatever God's plan is (no matter how ridiculous), he will do it.

Moses realized: it's not about the stick, or even the unexpected instructions. It's about the One who gave the instructions and promised to be faithful (1 Thessalonians 5:24).

If you want an expectation you can count on with God? Expect the unexpected. Embrace its purpose: to keep you safely focused on Who you can depend on, instead of relying on smooth sailing or logic for peace.

PRACTICE, PRACTICE, PRACTICE

Unexpected occasions allow us to practice what we are learning, if we can recognize the opportunity. Just as stillness increases our ability to see God in these situations (Psalm 46:10), fear and panic reduce our ability to interpret the real purpose of God at these times. So, God compassionately allows us to experience various training grounds where we can practice our peace in the midst of turmoil. These equipping sessions are crucial to our growth, because that's where we discover how many of our concepts of Him have actually become our reality. God is never disappointed if we discover that it's not as many as we thought, because He already knows where we truly stand. He is just kind enough to make sure that we understand it, too, so that we can embark on the next part of our development without getting ourselves (or someone else) seriously wounded in the process due to our well-intentioned ignorance.

Some days, Jesus' disciples feel like my own personal support group, encouraging me that there's a learning curve in this journey. My favorite story is in Mark 4 about their training opportunity during the storm on the lake. After a long day of parables, they piled into a boat and Jesus set the course: "We're going to the other side." Then He promptly went to sleep on a pillow (Mark 4:38). I love the pillow! It's a seemingly irrelevant detail that conveys so much. Jesus wasn't just crashed out after a long day of ministry; He was really, comfortably snuggled in, totally at rest.

Meanwhile, the storm kicked up and the boys began to become anxious, which means that it had to be a pretty rough storm. Half of them had grown up on that lake and were professional fishermen—they knew how to handle themselves when the waves got big. But that night, during that storm, their best determination was that they were sinking fast and Jesus didn't care. "C'mon Lord! This is no time to go to sleep on the job! We need You to do one of those miracle things!" No doubt Jesus just burrowed into His pillow a little deeper. He knew it was the perfect time to be unavailable. Why?

Because it was their turn. It was time to practice.

This was the next installment of their training and at least their second opportunity to put their experience of God into action. They'd had a previous occasion when 5000 people showed up to hear Jesus—5000 *hungry* people. When the disciples suggested to Jesus that the people should go away and get something to eat, Jesus said, "They do not need to go away. You give them something to eat" (Matthew 14:16). The disciples protested, pointing out how little they had (five loaves and two fish), so Jesus proceeded to demonstrate how to make it more than enough. He had given them an opportunity to practice, and they had decided to pass.

But Jesus had no intention of letting them become completely dependent on Him to do *all* the work, because He knew that He wasn't always going to be physically with them. Very soon, they would need to be able to connect with the Father in the same way that He did. In only a few months, He was no longer going to be physically visible to them (even though He would actually be more present than ever in their lives). So, the Lord left open spaces for them to practice taking responsibility for using what they had learned from Him. When this training opportunity came around, Jesus made Himself seemingly unavailable. The disciples would each face far worse than a storm one day, and He loved them too much to not give them the opportunity to take their best shot at releasing Papa's peace into their circumstances out of their own relationship with the Father, not His.

Jesus had previously taught them about who would endure in the Kingdom: those who both heard His words *and did them* (Luke 6:47). In this parable, Jesus described two men who both built houses, which were probably equally excellent in outward appearance. But the foundations of the houses were greatly different. Jesus described the man who both heard truth and took action as having created a foundation that would withstand the storm. Before the weather ever turned nasty, that man put the weight of practice on his revelations to see how much of them he had actually become. Truth wasn't just a concept to him; it was a rock-solid reality. Any gaps in his relationship with God were discovered ahead of time and could be filled accordingly.

The other man's house probably didn't seem much different — until the storm hit. No matter how excellent the construction of his home, his lack of foundation left it vulnerable to adversity. Once the waves began to pound and the winds began to blow, it was too late to apply the action which would have secured the faith and trust needed for a storm-weathering foundation.

For the disciples on the lake, Jesus was offering a surprise session of "Life with God: 101." It was time for them to discover if they had built a foundation on the rock of *their* relationship with the Father, or if their foundation was on the sandy soil of another's revelation that had not become their personal reality.

I've often wondered: what if Peter, James, John & Co. had reacted differently? What if they had recognized their opportunity to practice what they'd learned? I imagine one of them speaking up. "Hey guys, let's surprise Him! We've watched Him do the miracles, and we've done a few ourselves. The Father is bigger than this storm, right?" The other disciples nodded in agreement. "Remember that man who built his house on the rock? He survived a storm like this because he didn't just hear the Word — he did it. Let's do it! Let's release the peace of God into this storm by speaking to it."

Who knows which one of them would have said the actual words? Maybe they all would have declared peace together. But we'll never know what could have happened, because that night? They missed it. They lost their opportunity to personally speak to the storm, to let their relational peace surpass the natural power of the waves. They never got to see the look that would have been on Jesus' face when He would have opened His eyes, winked at them, and said, "Good job boys. You're getting it!"

That night on the lake, Jesus finally had to abandon His comfy pillow and remind them that they only needed a little bit of faith. He spoke to the storm and stilled it, showing once more what happens when life on earth is as it is in Heaven.

True to the gracious and patient nature of God, there would be other occasions in the disciples' futures when the unexpected was happening, and they would be given another chance to take action using what they had learned, combined with Who the Father had become to them. Though the Gospels show us that they missed several opportunities, they would eventually become champions with the help of the Holy Spirit. It's highly encouraging to me that the guys who turned the world upside down didn't get it right the first time through — or the second, or even the third. But they still got it…because they had been (and stayed) with Jesus (Acts 4:13).

FREEDOM FROM EXPECTATIONS

Expectations are overturned by the unexpected. If we've anchored our faith and peace only in thinking that we know what to expect and what will happen, we're in for a difficult journey. Expectancies can be subtle and tempting to hold on to for security. And when they become chained to opinions, it's easy for us to become thoroughly convinced that we know not only what should happen, but when and how too — not only in our own lives, but in the lives of those around us. That's unsteady ground, and we're likely to suffer the shipwreck of offense and disappointment when our anchor of expectation doesn't hold.

These presumptions can lead us to confining God and inadvertently manipulating His higher ways to fit our lesser ones. Emotional and spiritual blinders may form, limiting the range of His sovereignty. Under duress, we fail to see His hand at work. We can become deterred from our destiny because things don't appear to be happening the way we thought they would. Disillusionment begins to pull us away from the very path that God has meticulously designed for us — the path that will build the wisdom, endurance, and capacity we will need to live the life He intended.

In the Bruce Willis movie, "Live Free or Die Hard," cyber terrorists scramble every automated system in New York City. The subways are stopped. Computers are down. The traffic lights are out, and the streets are one big road accident, with cars piled on top of cars. The noise is deafening. Cell phones aren't working, and there's no 911 to call. Bruce emerges from an underground station and sees the massive mayhem for the first time. Everyone around him is lost in their own drama, yelling at the person who wrecked their car or panicking because they can't call a loved one. Instead of focusing on the chaos, Bruce leaps on top of a truck and surveys the scene. He isn't rushed. He takes his time. For me, the look on his face clearly communicates his thinking: "What's really going on here?" (Well, being Bruce Willis, that probably wasn't exactly what he was thinking… but that's my sanctified version.) Above the turmoil, he is looking beyond the obvious, searching for the common factor behind these apparently random incidents.

As I was processing that thought during the movie, the Holy Spirit jumped up inside me. "THAT'S your question! Whenever you are surrounded by chaos, ask Me, 'What's really going on here?' Don't focus on solving each ground level issue. Get above the individual drama and look at the big picture. I'll show you. Don't assume that you know the full story, and don't try to guess what's going to happen next."

It has indeed become my go to question. It's saved me from thinking that the battle I need to fight is the one I can clearly see, or that the fight is with other humans or against circumstances. And when I forget to ask it and charge ahead? Well, the results are usually unfortunate.

Make an intentional choice to lose your expectations of how circumstances will (or should) unfold. Use every unexpected occasion as an opportunity to practice letting go of the security of your plan. Climb with the Holy Spirit above your assumptions, opinions, and other people's bad behavior. Ask for His perspective: "What's really going on here?" The answer will often surprise you.

DAYS OF GRACE

When we become Joyfully Intentional people, our passion for development is so strong that we become fearless when investigating the lessons and opportunities to be gained in any situation, even if it's one in which we weren't at our best or events were unexpectedly tough. We are at rest in the grace of God. We understand that the first time we do anything, we're probably going to learn how not to do it.

Instead of bemoaning everything that went wrong, we automatically ask, "What can I learn?"

As a former performance junkie, this has been one of my greatest challenges. I was happy to love the learning when it was connected with something that I felt resulted in a grand success. But if I had just crashed and burned — if my actions had harmed others or I had been ridiculously self-focused instead of being God conscious — I had a difficult time loving the learning.

Thankfully, I've experienced continuing freedom in this area after hearing one of the most brilliant Graham Cooke thoughts ever: "What if there aren't good days or bad days, but only Days of Grace?"

Could God's grace really be that expansive? Could He really swallow up my stupidity with the same passion that He celebrated my victories? And could I believe it enough to actually love the learning on days I wished I could forget?

Yes.

In God's grace, we can stand and grow, win and lose, live and learn. It's a grace that abounds, exceeds, and is abundant (Ephesians 3:20) — so much so that almost every apostle began and ended his letters with a desire that the readers would have a profound revelation of it. It is a gift, not a goal — a gift that expands peace, truth, and hope beyond all reason. Grace has made us accepted in the Beloved and rich in His kindness. Combined with faith, it is how we are saved from an old life of trying to be good into a new life of living in the One Who is goodness itself.

When even a small portion of that truth becomes our reality, every situation we encounter becomes a condemnation-free learning experience (whether it's expected or unexpected). We can celebrate where we've seen our evidences of transformation. Like well-loved children, we can come boldly, bounding in to the Throne of Grace in times of need (Hebrews 4:16). If we did or said things that hurt another, we can't wait to meet God's grace-filled eyes, honestly say, "I'm sorry," and then go and express the same to our friend. We recognize that the goodness of God has made us stronger in the places we might have fallen before, and we can be thankful when we see the gaps that still remain — knowing that the provision to overcome in those areas is also there in Christ. We can abandon the exhausting roller coaster of *good* and *bad* days, exchanging them for the broad, ever-upward highway that Days of Grace reveal.

And so far, I feel as if I am barely ankle deep in the ocean of God's grace that is there to experience. It's stretches beyond what I can see, what I can imagine…but I am looking forward to diving in even deeper. On this journey, it doesn't matter if the twists and turns are known or unknown. Every day will end the same as it began: full of grace, full of possibilities, and full of promise. The only real expectancy that we ever need to have is the joy of knowing that tomorrow, we will encounter God in His grace and goodness once again.

Mindset #3: The Unexpected Is to Be Expected

1. When was the last time you were disappointed by an unexpected event or unexpected action by a friend or family member?

2. Did you have expectations that were not met? How about opinions regarding what should have occurred that didn't? How might that have contributed to your response?

3. Could you exchange some of those expectations of people and circumstances for an expectation of who God wants to be to you in those places?

4. Take a moment to walk through those situations again in your mind, this time expecting who God wants to be for you in that situation instead. How would that change your story in a way that would better equip you for future unexpected times?

MINDSET #4:
MINERS AND TREASURE HUNTERS

I've lived in or near a Sierra Nevada gold rush town for over thirty years.
I have friends who are active gold miners, and there are days when I
can hear the mining equipment that still works the creek near my house.
Several years ago, my husband and I spent two separate vacations
exploring every inch of Highway 49 and the history of the California
Mother Lode. They were two of our best trips ever.

I not only love the stories of the California Gold Rush, but the Holy Spirit
has continually used them to creatively teach me about the Joyful Intentionality of valuing, collecting, and processing the treasure God gives us.
Several of the activations included in the second half of this book come
out of what He's taught me through those stories.

In my travels, I discovered that many of the people who came to California in 1849 thought they would find gold just laying about on the
ground. That belief was so strong that a unique product described as
"Gold Salve" became a popular item. According to its inventors, all a
person had to do to collect their fortune was simply smear themselves
with the sticky salve, toss themselves on the ground, and roll around.
They'd stand up, covered in gold and instant riches with very little effort.

More than likely, you're laughing at the idea (both at the product and the
purchasers). I thought it was funny, too…until I realized that my basic
approach to revelation from God had been quite similar to "Gold Salve"
for many years. I thought that if I simply slathered myself in conferences

or books, the truth they contained would magically stick to me, providing me with tremendous wealth in the mysteries of the Kingdom.

But, just like "Gold Salve," that's not quite how it works.

Revelation can be imparted in a Spirit-filled atmosphere or an A-ha! moment, but that impartation is like discovering a gold vein in a rock or gold dust in a stream: you have it, but it still needs to be intentionally collected and processed. There are many different ways to process truth, and none of them are *right* or *wrong* in and of themselves. You just have to know which tools to use and which processes match the type of deposit you are developing.

THE PANNING PROCESS

Some truths cannot be grasped quickly. Mysteries and wisdom especially need intentional exploration and development to be fully revealed. Like a miner panning for gold in a river, we may take in a lot of teaching, but it is our persistent process of swirling it around and around in Living Water that allows what has weight and value to settle and become evident. It takes time for deep truth to emerge and even longer for it to become part of who we are, not just what we know.

Meditation is like the gold panning process to me. Times of meditation are when I take a thought that God has deposited in me through Scripture, teaching, or prayer, and think deeply with Him about it. I ask Him questions and keep on discovering how to ask better and better questions. I seek who He is for me in this truth and delightfully keep on seeking. I knock at the doors that He is unlocking and keep on knocking in the quiet confidence that what I'm exploring will become more and more clear as we process it together. During this time, I don't try to connect all the dots; I'm just collecting them. I keep short notes so that I don't lose the brilliant thoughts that emerge, but I don't try to dig through the dirt to pull out the nuggets just yet.

Time in worship, contemplation, and stillness will eventually reveal the treasure. God loves these relational times, so He is rarely in a hurry to rush through them. What is revealed will be uncovered gradually. It won't be all in one lump, but that doesn't make it any less valuable. Just like the gold flakes sifted by the miner in his panning process, it is the accumulated weight of revelation that becomes the treasure.

THE PICKAXE

Other truths won't magically unfold or be discovered in their entirety without active digging. We may find evidence of a vein of revelation, but we will have to dig to discover where it leads. Old mindsets that get in the way will become evident as we go and will require consistent, active, intentional chipping away using the pickaxe of truth, powered by the grace of what God is revealing instead.

When I find myself in this type of process, I am intentional to keep the truth I'm mining before me, so that I'm connecting with it throughout my day. I will post it on my bathroom mirror or on the bulletin board in my office. When I see it, I remember to smile at the Holy Spirit, my Teacher, who knows all the secrets that we will discover together. If a brilliant thought occurs to me, I'll take a moment to jot it down. After I've taken initial notes about the truth that has captivated my attention, I look for other entries in my journals that may hold clues from past explorations.

Hunting through the Bible for Scriptures that enlighten and expand my understanding is always a part of my digging deeper. In the excavating process, it's helpful to actively thank God that we have the Mind of Christ about the truth that's being revealed, declaring our confidence that we will see it through His eyes and hear it through His ears, perceiving it as He does. This thankfulness is especially helpful when what we are pursuing seems to lack clarity. It helps us to remain at rest, knowing that as we keep digging, the truth that we're contemplating will become more and more focused.

In the hard rock gold mines of the west, miners often sang as they labored, creating a sense of camaraderie and a rhythm for their work through music. The work was challenging, but their songs and fellowship allowed them to remain focused on the worthwhile rewards that lay before them. They encountered a variety of obstacles, but the best mining crews found ways to overcome them by working together. Excavating truth can take persistence, but when we keep a song of thankfulness in our hearts and involve our friends in our process, the shared experience becomes joyful. Great conversations with others that are following a similar vein of truth can be wonderful for this type of processing because they allow us to encourage each other when the going gets tough and the dust of digging obscures the pursuit of our reward — to know God in the fullness of who He really is and our true identity in Christ.

And while we're swinging the pickaxe of process, once again, we remain in peace. Truths like these will take time to unfold. The revelation we are following probably won't open up in a day or a week. It may take months to follow to its source, but that's okay. As we go, we're relationally building joyful endurance, stamina, and focus as we follow the vein — which is always a cause for rejoicing. Remember: we are working in partnership with the One who knows where all the treasures are buried!

DYNAMITE

Sometimes, however, you're not panning or digging. There are occasions when God suddenly shows up and blows up your world with a truth so explosive that it shatters your old mindsets and perceptions in one fell swoop. Everything disappears in a cloud of dust, as you realize that what you thought was true isn't the Truth. For a while, it's hard to tell up from down. Majesty overwhelms everything and takes your breath away.

The first thing I do when I experience one of these "suddenlies" is to just be still. I don't try to figure things out or take action. There's too many rocks of revelation still falling for it to be safe to move! I wait for the dust to clear. Once it does, I can get a look at what's been uncovered. Was there an obstacle that this Truth annihilated? What new mother lode of promises or provision did it reveal?

Dynamite revelations move the most ground the quickest, but they usually leave the biggest piles of sorting and processing. Some explosive truths can take months or even years to sift through. While they can be impressive in their impact, be prepared to roll up your sleeves for a while and work in partnership with the Holy Spirit to sort through the deposit that's left behind.

After miners used dynamite to go deeper into a mountain, they still employed the techniques of crushing and eventually sifting with water in order to locate the precious ore. Massive downloads still need refining.

Stillness and meditation are required after the explosion has separated the precious from the common to reveal the full potential of wisdom and mysteries that God's "suddenly" has made available.

TREASURE IS WORTH IT

The treasure of revelation is quite exciting, but the process of making it part of our lives certainly sounds like a lot of work, inconvenience, mess, and effort. And in many ways, it is!

The California miners of 1849 discovered this quickly. Panning gold for ten minutes is fun. Crouching all day in cold water—swirling dirt around for eight to ten hours—takes stamina. Swinging a pickaxe takes muscle. And blasting with dynamite takes courage, followed by a great deal of effort in excavation.

So, why do it? Because it's GOLD!

People didn't rush from all over the world to California in 1849 because they discovered granite, obsidian, or sand. Gold has value. And when something has great value, it's worth going after with everything you have. That's the whole premise of the parable about the Pearl of Great Price: you commit your life to the search, selling everything you have when you find it—because it's worth it.

Like the miners of old, we joyfully cultivate hearts that recognize truth and wisdom. We learn where treasure is most likely to be hidden. (Adversity is a top contender. So is the unexpected and the delayed.) Like the miners who watched flooded rivers carefully each Spring to see where the pounding high waters would slam into the riverbanks and tree roots (depositing precious nuggets of gold in the process that could be mined when the waters calmed), we discern where the challenges in our lives have deposited revelation that we can explore later. We develop patience to wait for the floods of adversity to recede, knowing that something well worth uncovering is waiting to be found.

Casual pursuit or wishful thinking won't be enough. We'll need to make the choice to pay the price, making a plan to pursue our discoveries through intentionally giving our time and focus to growing up into all things in Christ. When we find the next "X" on our spiritual treasure map, we understand that the real process is just beginning — not ending.

I have a friend named Tim who is a professional mining engineer. He told me the story of some men who purchased a copper mine that everyone thought was depleted. The previous owners had dug exploratory holes to see if there was more copper below, but they came up empty. Yet, these men believed there was more, so they bought the property for a very low price. Sure enough, by choosing to dig even deeper, the men uncovered an enormous horizontal shelf of copper that was ten times the size of the original, vertical vein that the previous owners had followed! So, even when you've already dug deeply, always venture deeper still. You never know what astonishing treasure a little more patience and perseverance may uncover.

Gold Rush miners kept their hard-earned, precious gold dust and nuggets very close, usually in a leather pouch worn as a necklace that they never took off. When we discover Truth, we don't just leave it laying around either. Our notes and journals are treated with care. We develop strategies to continually refine, develop, and review what we've uncovered. We have a passion to be like the Good Steward of Matthew 25, caring for what's been entrusted to us, knowing that faithful stewardship opens the door to be given more.

In 1849, stories of the California Gold Rush stirred up lots of excitement back East, but the only ones who earned the true 49ers name were the people with the courage to actually make the journey across the country into what was then relatively uncharted territory. Sometimes you may need to include travel as part of your spiritual quest for the treasure that God has waiting for you. Over the years, I've taken many trips, pursuing and exploring with God (sometimes at significant expense) because actually being in the atmosphere of certain cities, meetings, teachings, and worship was worth it to me. Sure, I could have checked out a travelogue or have gotten the CDs later. I had the option to wait and hope that the teacher I wanted to learn from would come to a location near me. But there are moments in time and atmospheres I have experienced firsthand that literally changed everything in my life. There are some personal encounters that I'm still mining over a decade later. I've never regretted the investment in travel when I knew I was supposed to be there.

PROGRAMS FOR COMPLETION OR A PROCESS THAT MAKES US RICH

Shortly after the announcement of the discovery of gold in California, a variety of guidebooks flooded the market, offering readers tips on how to get to the gold fields quickly and the easy ways to discover rich deposits. Ironically, the vast majority of these guidebooks were written by people who had never actually ventured west of the Mississippi River themselves. The readers who eagerly followed their instructions found that their results ranged from simply discovering that their guidebook was unhelpful to experiencing truly tragic outcomes as they followed its directions. (The Donner Party was one of those.)

"Programs" can range from step-by-step instructions that promise instant, almost miraculous outcomes in everything from weight loss to spiritual maturity; to those that offer solid information and skills. The quick-fix programs give a sense of "Follow our easy steps and these results are guaranteed," except that it rarely works that way. Legitimate study programs can offer education, but they may be the only construct we've experienced for development. The key here is understanding that Christian programs and the process of growing up into all things in Christ (Ephesians 4:15) are not automatically the same thing and that it's important to consider the differences.

Here's some of what we've discovered in creating a process-based environment for spiritual development:

Programs are often designed with the goal of behavioral change. A lifestyle of process is focused on transformation into the image of Christ.

Programs traditionally teach what to think. Process coaches and encourages us in *how* to think.

Programs provide direct instruction with a defined curriculum. Process uses instruction as only one of several tools to cultivate growth, and allows for feedback, dialogue, questions and adjustments. Upgrades to the process can be offered by both members and leaders, and are made based on what we learn as we travel together.

Programs often rely on deadlines for motivation.
Process desires to create inspiration that produces passion to take action.

Programs utilize questions to determine if the information has been learned.
Process uses questions for exploration, prompting new thoughts for continuing contemplation in context of relationship with God.

Programs are often prescriptive towards the goal of a specific outcome.
Process is descriptive of the variety of riches to be gathered on a progressive journey.

Programs generally value comprehension of the material as evidence of completion.
Process values evidences of transformation: how our perceptions, thinking, and behavior have become more like Christ and our resulting stories that demonstrate our experiences.

Programs are usually self-contained. The answers to the questions are most likely in the materials that are included.
In a process environment, our learning is experiential as well as conceptual and answers are often found in our real-world experiences as much as in the materials we use.

Programs create community connections often based on the shared material or work done together.
Process creates friendships as you walk with fellow travelers, overcoming obstacles and banding together to make your way through previously undiscovered country.

There are, of course, programs that have been written by those who have authentically travelled the territory for themselves. There are study courses that people have participated in which have had a wonderful impact on their lives or that have created precious friendships. I'm not saying that those things can't occur in a traditional program. But consider a relational, exploratory style of process as another option to what may have been our previous corporate experiences as we go looking for God's treasures together.

THE REAL TREASURE OF THE PROCESS

It wasn't just their acquisition of gold that the 49ers valued after they became old men. Most of them never found a Mother Lode, yet they reflected on their days of mining and exploration with great affection. Besides gold, they had discovered another treasure in the process, one that made them rich.

According to their journals, many of them had made their way to California because they felt that, if God was leaving gold just laying around, they had a Divine responsibility to go get it. Of course there were those who went West only to get rich quick, but for the most part, many families back East sacrificed to send their loved one into the unknown in hopes of gaining security (not wealth) for their families. Yet, few returned home with either one, so why did they speak so fondly of this time in their lives? Numerous records exist that were written by people who grew up listening to the tales told by a real 49er (their Grandpa or a great uncle) as they sat together on their front porch. As you read them, you discover that there seemed to be a universal pride and fraternity among those that had ventured West, even though they may have returned home with seemingly little to show for it.

When asked about their experiences, their replies were quite similar. It had been the adventure of a lifetime. The wonders they had seen, the adversities they had overcome, and the friends that they made along the way had become the true treasure of their lives.

For me, those recollections offer the ultimate example of how it is truly the process that enriches us. It is not only what we discover in truth and revelation but also the wealth of the journey together with God and with our friends that provides us the greatest riches of all.

Most treasures won't come to us. We'll need to actively go out asking, seeking and knocking. But we have something the 49ers didn't have: a promise that if we ask, seek and knock, we will uncover what God has for us. And in addition to outstanding revelation, the relational reward of our intentional search and commitment to processing what we find will be lasting and rich.

Mindset #4: Miners and Treasure Hunters

1. What is a current revelation that you want to explore more?

2. Is it a truth that requires meditation?

3. Are there old mindsets that need to be displaced first or unlearned?

4. Has God recently blown up your world with an expansive insight?

5. Or is the revelation a combination of all of the above?

6. If you don't have a current truth that you are excavating, is there one that you'd like to begin exploring now? If so, how will you begin?

MINDSET #5:
LIFE BEYOND THE COMFORT ZONE

I was raised to be safe and predictable. Risk taking was not part of my family's culture—especially my Dad's. My father worked as an architect for the city of Los Angeles for 44 years. Straight lines, precise measurements, and job security were his standard operating procedures. His idea of a vacation was going to the same place (San Diego), to the same motel (Motel 6 at the Taylor Street off ramp), eating breakfast at the same place every morning (Ricky's), and visiting the same attractions on the same day, year after year (Monday: the Zoo; Tuesday: Sea World; Wednesday: Coronado; Thursday: the San Diego Air & Space Museum....) You get the idea.

Yes... the same vacation every year. There were a few exceptions early on, but after a while, San Diego and "vacation" were one and the same. When I was 10 years old, my parents asked if I would feel left out if they went to San Diego while I was at church camp. I knew that it was important to look as if I was mildly disappointed, but not so disappointed that they would abandon the idea. Apparently, I struck the right note, because San Diego had to do without me that year. And each summer after, I graciously volunteered to continue to make this grand sacrifice—thereby avoiding San Diego throughout the rest of my adolescence while simultaneously garnering the acclaim of my family for my selfless actions. Pretty brilliant, huh?

Otherwise, my very predictable life continued down its very predictable pathway, until the day that a letter came in the mail that offered me (a

48

soon-to-be college freshman) an opportunity to study abroad in Germany for a year. While I longed to travel, I couldn't imagine my Dad saying "Yes" to another continent when he couldn't say "Yes" to another city for vacation...even if he wasn't the one going. Germany? Not a chance.

I was about to throw the letter away when my mother asked what it was. I handed it to her. She read it carefully and slowly. When she was finished reading, she simply asked, "Do you want to go?"

"Of course I want to go!" was my automatic reply. "But Dad will never say 'Yes' to this!"

Once again, my mom re-read the letter intently. Then, raising her eyes from the page and with a resolve that I had never seen before, she quietly said, "Your father will agree to it."

To this day, I have no idea what she said to convince him, but he said "Yes." Thanks, Mom.

Suddenly the nineteen year-old who had never travelled outside of Southern California was off to the other side of the world—and I've never looked back. While everyone else was saying tearful good-byes at the airport, I couldn't wait to start the adventure. And while my classmates got homesick after several months, I was trying to figure out how to stay longer. I loved my family, but somehow, I was at home in the unknown, far away from my comfort zone of predictability.

"FOLLOW ME"

Leaving my comfort zone hasn't just been true for travel. There have been times where I had to choose between a financially secure job and an opportunity that I felt was the next part of my destiny. I've made some uncomfortable choices to say "No" to expected relationships and "Yes" to surprising ones. Often, there have not been safety nets or fall back plans to make the decision easier, just the smile of the Father and an assurance of His faithfulness.

**When Jesus said "Follow Me" to the Disciples,
it wasn't a one-time instruction. He was letting**

**them know that life with Him would be a continuing
process of choosing to go (or not go) where He was going.**

Jesus didn't set up a home base and stay there during his three and a half years of ministry. He was always moving about—teaching on a mountain top one day, in the synagogue the next afternoon, and around a dinner table that night. Along the way, He was healing people, multiplying food, and making house calls. Never once do we hear Him laying out His plan for the next month, making sure that everyone was okay with it. It wasn't always safe to be with Jesus, and there certainly was no guessing what would happen next. But, without a doubt, it was totally worth the risk for those who took the opportunity to follow Him.

And it's still the same today. Each of us will still have to intentionally choose to follow an always faithful God who is famous for His unpredictable actions. Our Comfort Zones will need to be continuously traded for The Comforter. We will risk looking inept at times and all of our insecurities will rush to the surface in an attempt to convince us that the perils are too great. We're certain to fail miserably on occasion, because we aimed high—and missed. The Gospels are full of people like that. But the Bible also tells us that, by walking with Jesus down all those unlikely roads headed to unexpected places, the Disciples were transformed into men who would turn the world upside down because they had risked everything to be with Him—and, in the process, had become amazingly like Him.

JUMP WHILE YOU CAN

Moving beyond the Comfort Zone isn't just about saying "Yes" to an adventure; it's also knowing when to say it. Years ago, I thought that I had all the time in the world and that the options before me would always be available. I was willing to follow God, but often I wanted it to be on my schedule, not His. I hadn't realized yet that opportunity and risk are partners.

**An intentional response to God is required based on
the fact that the opportunity is here today—
not because we know the details of tomorrow.**

50

"When the opportunity of a lifetime comes, we must respond within the lifetime of the opportunity." This quote from Graham Cooke has had a profound impact on my life. My choices are to be fully based on His "Yes," not on my complete understanding. It is one of our greatest acts of worship to say to the Lord, "I trust You" — not only with our words, but with our actions.

The Bible is filled with people who opened the Door of Opportunity when God came knocking and we can be encouraged by their stories. Moses said "Yes" at the Burning Bush, giving us hope that even reluctant agreement can start the adventure of a lifetime. The boy, Samuel, showed us that years of experience are not always necessary. He said "Yes" to a voice in the night...and ended up listening for a nation the rest of his days. Peter chose the option of getting out of the boat when he heard, "Come." And, though he ended up getting a little wet, the risk was worth it. Jesus never made the offer again, and the Disciples who reasonably stayed put would never know what it felt like to walk on water.

Gideon, Caleb, David, Esther, Nehemiah, Mary, John, Paul...the list goes on and on of those who took the risk — who said "Yes" to an opportunity of a lifetime within the lifetime of that opportunity.

What would have happened if Moses had continued to resist the strong voice of the Lord until the bush flames out? What if Peter, John, and James had placed more faith in their Fisherman's Union 401k than the vague invitation of a carpenter from Nazareth? What if Esther had thought her Uncle Mordecai was overreacting? Or if David had listened to the military experts about Goliath?

There is no doubt that God's will and purposes will be accomplished. It is not that it won't happen without us, but rather that it's God's delight to do it with us.

No one jumps out of an airplane that is sitting on the ground and proudly posts the video on Facebook. Sure, there is a guarantee of a safe landing, but what would be the point? God straps us into the parachute of His true nature, takes us up in His aircraft of possibilities, and pushes back the Door of Opportunity. As the wind rushes in, it's time to choose.

The plane won't stay in the sky forever.

That thought has made me purposely jump from my safe places many times now. And though it has yet to be comfortable, I've come to expect the inevitable free fall into the unknown. I know the chute will open — though it sometimes opens later than I would have preferred.

Do I dive fearlessly into every divine opportunity or always recognize its knock? Not yet.

I still go through a process, moving from recognition to relentless trust; but my travel time is far less than it used to be because I've had a taste of the outcomes that can follow. I now will intentionally say "Yes" based on that alone. If He's going, so am I.

It's a quality that I think all Joyfully Intentional people embrace strongly. They take risks on purpose because they know it's part of a brilliant journey. God makes no promises about an easy or predictable life. But He does promise that He will always be with us and that *He* will never change — which makes rest and risk great partners in the Kingdom. Our circumstances are not guaranteed, but our relationship with God is. So, be at peace…and jump!

DO I REALLY HAVE PERMISSION?

"How do I know if God is saying 'Yes'?" is a question I had for years and hear often from others. For me, the answer has come from one of my key Inheritance Scriptures, Isaiah 30. The first words that God highlighted to me in this passage were in verse 21: "Your ears shall hear a word behind you saying, 'This is the way, walk in it'…." I spent a great deal of time meditating on that phrase as my life continued to move from one leap of faith to the next, as I trusted His promise that I would hear His guiding Voice.

But it wasn't until several months after He initially highlighted this truth that I began to comprehend the second half of the verse: "Your ears shall hear a word behind you saying, 'This is the way, walk in it', *whenever you turn to the right hand or the left.*" How could I have missed that? Based on relationally walking with Him, I have God's permission to continue to move forward at all times, responding to the next direction He initiates.

If I veer off to one side or the other, *then* He will use His voice to give me the course correction that I need. I cooperate with Him by maintaining a sensitive ear in my worship, meditation, and prayers, but I shouldn't need five prophetic words, two angelic appearances, and a note in a bottle for confirmation!

When I get off track, He has promised to give a shout: "Hey, Al! Sweetheart...not that way. Come over here." Sometimes His voice comes through circumstances that He allows—the very ones that I often see as obstacles. He loves to use these circumstances as occasions to show me a "...more excellent way" (I Corinthians 12:31). I think I give God a great deal of amusement as I storm the heavens attempting to overcome something that He is happily waiting for me to realize is simply the redirection that I need. And if I'm really being thick, He'll send along a friend (who usually knows nothing about my situation) to speak words of life on His behalf. Often, they will use familiar words or even exact phrases from my times of prayer to signal from God, "Pay attention, Allison. This is Me."

Times like that make me feel loved, safe, and secure—not ashamed. I have no plans or expectations to be right 100% of the time. And, while I certainly don't want to put the job of correcting my course on my friends or on prophetic ministers, I remain willing to take risks, because I know the weight of being on target isn't all on me. I sincerely want to keep a sensitive ear so that, when God nudges me to the left or to the right, I shift easily. But I can be at rest in the knowledge that, if I miss it, He is faithful to speak loud and clear. And if I really miss it, then I will still have the experience of His grace to illuminate and fill my vulnerable places. There's something so incredibly humbling and profound about God's kindness on your most idiotic days. It's not my preferred method of maturity, but it's probably the one I am most grateful for.

Because God's words prepare and illuminate a way for us to walk in (Psalm 119:105), He wants us to confidently step forward into the opportunities that He brings.

It is part of becoming a mature son or daughter of God to not need constant affirmation or confirmation—but to instead demonstrate trust in the nature of God for us and the permission He has given us to explore the Kingdom. We love being loved by Him and loving Him in return, so it is our good pleasure to go where He is going, stop when He is stopping, and run when He is running. Course corrections are part of any journey; we can expect and embrace them as the acts of love that they are. The rest of the time, we travel in the peace of His dependability to keep us on track as needed.

When Comfort Zones Are Exchanged for The Comforter

When we personally experience the Holy Spirit as The Comforter, then *He* becomes our comfort zone. Risk taking shifts to being part of everyday life in God—not an event, nor a story from long ago, but part of a normal Kingdom experience.

The dreamers, heroes, and champions that I have the privilege of walking with in life rarely talk about taking risks. Instead, they speak about their next adventure with God. They know their promises, permissions, and are clear on His timing, so they've pushed all their chips into the middle of the table—"all in" when it comes to doing what God has said to do. It's an astounding act of worship: trusting that—no matter how high the stakes may have seemed in the process—when the last card is played, it will be the enemy who has the tables turned on him. As overcomers in Christ, the only way we lose is if we fold, giving in to the intimidation of circumstances before God makes His final move. It takes courage to stay at the table (especially when the Lord ups the ante at the most illogical times) but the experience of seeing the look on the enemy's face when he is defeated—yet again—is priceless. Not only have we achieved the victory, but in the process, we've become stronger, wiser, more peaceful and confident in who God is for us—better equipped when the next round of circumstances is dealt.

This is not a life of Pollyanna thinking or one of reckless action. I am quite realistic about the cost on days in finances, time, development and sacrifice; but the alternative of mediocrity seems a far higher price to pay. Excellence is a reasonable service to an excellent God. Any loss pales to the gains that are on offer in Christ (Philippians 3:8).

More and more, we find a deepening security in the reality of promises that require faith and patience (Hebrews 6:12). As we journey together, we're becoming a growing community that is being drawn into a relational process, invited to really know the Holy Spirit in His nature as the Comforter — until He is more real than whatever faces us. God's promises are heard as His language of consolation, support, assurance, cheer, and love.

We are learning how to speak God's language of promise to a world whose tangible assurances are rapidly vanishing.

These are not words that are platitudes, but a rich sound that has the depth that only comes from personal encounter with the Living Word (John 1:1).

I once asked an ex-inmate friend why she continued to listen to me when she was on the processing yards of the prison where we held regular services. My physical appearance, no matter how casually I dressed, clearly indicated that we came from very different worlds. I wasn't a very polished speaker at the time. Everyone else in the ministry seemed far more gifted than I was… so I wondered. When I asked her about it, she replied, "It was the sound of your voice…and the authenticity in your eyes. You see, on the streets, I lived or died by knowing if people were telling me the truth. It wasn't what you said, but how you said it. I knew the words were true because of the sound that they had. You had experienced the God you were talking about. He was real — and your eyes confirmed it."

It was then that I realized that the language of God has a certain sound to it: a resonance of kindness, comfort, love, confidence, and grace…a sound that transcends visible opposition. It is stronger than just the theological content of what we're saying. When we've *become* a truth by encountering its reality in the midst of journeying through adversity with our Comforter and Friend, what we say has a transformational level of impact. It has the sound of authenticity that relational, Joyful Intentionality brings.

Earthbound levels of comfort are a cheap substitute for a relationship with The Comforter, so why settle for them? God isn't trying to take something away from us. He is graciously wanting to expand our lives into a dynamic relationship that will transcend any situation we encounter. It is often the very adversity or challenge that the enemy means to overwhelm us with becomes the stairway to an elevated relationship with the persona of the Holy Spirit as our Teacher, our Spirit of Truth, our Helper, Counselor, Intercessor, Advocate, Strengthener, and Standby Friend. (John 14:16-17, Amplified Bible). He's like a whole team of experts—full of wisdom, instruction, comfort, and cheer! And you can never lose Him, because He's in you wherever you go.

Comfort zone or The Comforter? It's not really a difficult decision. It's kind of like choosing between San Diego or Europe: I'll take the expansive adventure of a continent over a city any day, thank you very much!

And if there are times when all of that still isn't enough and I still feel torn between my earthly comfort zone and The Comforter, there's an image that always propels me in the right direction. That image is the thought of standing one day before Jesus and explaining that I chose the comfort zone over The Comforter because I was too scared or felt that I was too unqualified—pulling out a logical list of why His promises wouldn't have worked, trying to convince Him that my assessment of "impossible" was true. How absurd would that be...and yet I've thought like that more times than I care to remember. The Father has been endlessly patient when my prayers became more about bemoaning circumstances than remaining focused on my promises. He simply lets me see myself, standing face-to-face with His Son having this conversation; not aggravated in the least, just waiting for me to realize once again how ridiculous this scenario is.

Jesus intentionally gave up all the comforts of Heaven and willingly entered into our world in its cruelest form. That would have been sacrifice enough, but He continued on into hell itself, taking captivity captive (Ephesians 4:8) so that it would become a zone that we never had to experience. And when the joy set before Him (Hebrews 12:2) carried Him to the other side of His finish line, I can picture Him running to the Holy Spirit and shouting "Tag, You're it!" Now it's the Spirit's turn to invade our lives with truth, illumination, hope, revelation, and joy. And He's up for the adventure! The love for Him that those thoughts evoke fuels me to go forward, knowing that He will always be with me, even to the end of the age (Matthew 28:20).

I've spent time imagining God with Moses on the last day of Moses' life, as together they savored the deep friendship that began in reluctant obedience...the moment that Esther realized that slave girls really can change a nation...and have pictured Peter's amazement on the day of Pentecost.

I've imagined the end of my own life, too, and the smile on the face of Jesus because I responded to opportunities He gave me within the lifetime that they were available. When we stand before Jesus, we'll be glad we were prepared for leaps of faith and jumped—only to find again and again that we could depend on the parachute of His true nature and promises every time...and that life with The Comforter is better than a comfort zone any day.

Mindset #5: Life Beyond the Comfort Zone

1. What would you attempt for God if you knew you could not fail?

2. What is your greatest fear in undertaking something new, or something at a new level?

3. What is the comfort zone you are leaving?

4. Who will The Comforter be for you instead?

5. Is there a Scripture, promise, or prophecy for this new territory?

6. What is the sound of your current language in every day conversations? Is it filled with promises you've encountered — or with platitudes that you deeply wish were real in your experience?

7. Take time to listen to His way of speaking about that in His Word and in your heart. What is His tone? What are His promises to you?

MINDSET #6:
FINE-TUNING YOUR RECEIVER

On any given day, there are songs, laughter, and conversation all around you. In almost any room anywhere, music is playing. The only difference between hearing it or not is whether you have a radio that is tuned in so that you can listen. The sound exists, but it doesn't exist for you until you have a receiver that can pull it from the airwaves and broadcast it into your world.

> **Our first role in the Kingdom is to become excellent**
> ***receivers* of the love of God and of His true nature.**

Tuning in to God's conversation with us is an intentional, joyful action of fine-tuning our receivers to His frequency. On eight different occasions, the Gospels record Jesus saying, "For him who has ears to hear, let him hear." Apparently, just possessing these sound receptacles on the sides of our heads doesn't guarantee that we will hear with our hearts. We can recognize sounds and words, but "hearing" involves translating those sounds and words into understanding that creates lasting impact on our mindsets and perceptions. Lots of people heard the teachings of Jesus, but not everyone experienced transformation just by being present.

> **Joyful Intentionality takes the Truth that we've heard and**
> **allows us to keep hearing it and beholding God in it until we**
> **become like Him. But we need to fine tune our ears to hear**
> **Him in the first place in order for that process to begin.**

One of my favorite examples of the fine-tuning needed is recorded in John 12. The Father spoke audibly to Jesus, telling Him that His Name has been glorified and would be again. But some of the people near Jesus when this happened thought that it thundered, and others said that an angel had spoken to Him. One Voice was present, and Jesus heard it clearly — but those who were tuned into another frequency heard something very different. For them, there were no words to even consider processing.

Fine-tuning can be delightful and highly individual. I've found that God uses it all the time with those who have ears to hear, customizing what He wants to communicate to each person present during a teaching session. I'm always amazed as I talk with people after a meeting and discover all the different things they heard. Everyone was present for the same talk, but the truths that stand out to people are so wide and diverse! The Holy Spirit is a genius at highlighting exactly the right word for the right moment and connecting our dots as we listen with our hearts.

Others, however, exemplify the impact that distractions or distorted filters can have on what's received when compared to what was actually said. Old mindsets can twist a straightforward truth into a muddled message that bears little resemblance to what was actually said. Instead of hearing the clear sound of the Father in an excellent teaching, they perceive only vague religious rumblings and move on to the next event.

Even without these distortions, it is wise to listen to quality teachings again and again, so that we can pull out the wide variety of truths that we may have missed the first time. The points that were relevant when we initially encountered the message will shift as we grow and transform. We will not (hopefully) be the same person a year or two from now, so listening to a five-fold teaching twelve to twenty-four months later should be a different and worthwhile experience. Recently, a close friend quoted from a book that I'd been very familiar with for over ten years. In the words she read aloud, was a key revelation to an upgrade I'd felt a bit stuck in. I had read that book countless times and even used it in small groups for training, but when she quoted from it, my current circumstances had me tuned in to understand the truth in a totally new way.

**We grow more quickly when we don't always look for
our answers *out there*, but continue to intentionally
review what we've already received.**

And to all the teachers out there: it's good to remember that, just because
you said it, doesn't mean that people heard and understood it as you
anticipated. If it happened to the Father, it can surely happen to us.
We have the joy of finding lots of creative ways of expressing the same
concepts again and again, knowing that transformational understanding
is often a multi-dimensional process with truth, not a single encounter.
We choose patience instead of frustration when asked to share again
about what we thought was so crystal clear. We decide to be thankful
that people are pursuing understanding and hopefully, we ask them the
right questions that will facilitate their personal revelation.

OVERCOMING STATIC

Just like radio waves in the natural, there are conditions that can cause
interfering static in our perceptions of God and what He is saying. We
can develop filters that distort our hearing, much like lenses can alter our
vision. Untended hurts, performance mindsets, past experiences, and
future fears can turn the Father's affirmation into a vague sound that
doesn't hold much meaning for us. As we become more aware of our
internal static and filters, we cooperate with God in fine-tuning our inner
receiver and displacing our distortions.

A lifestyle of stillness and rest is the greatest key to clearing the airwaves
of our mind and soul so that we can clearly hear God's heart for us.
Fear, doubt, and worry create static which drowns out the very assurances we're listening for. Thanksgiving, worship, and praise create an
atmosphere for clarity; every time we fill our internal space with them,
our capacity to receive expands. In every circumstance, we choose what
station we will tune into: peace or worry, fear or perfect Love, unbelief
or trust.

THE CHANNEL AT THE END OF THE DIAL

One of the best encounters that I've experienced with fine-tuning my
own receiver was initially one of the most mystifying — as well as

amusing. It completely revolutionized how I interact with God, and it annihilated a number of religious filters in my perceptions.

Several years ago, I was at one of Graham Cooke's conferences when he gave a corporate prophetic word. I got the CD, went home, and transcribed it. There was one particular phrase of God's that leaped off the page to me. *"I do not seek your adoration. I seek your blessing."*

What did that mean? Didn't God love our adoration? That's what worship was all about, right? And how is that any different than blessing God? It didn't make any sense to me.

I pondered it every day for weeks, until it came time to attend the prophetic school that Graham held every six months (at that time) in Vancouver, Washington. This was perfect! It was a small venue that seated less than 100 people; surely I would be able to ask him what the phrase meant. (The prospect of an actual conversation with Graham was something that seemed overwhelming at the time, but at this point, getting an answer was worth overcoming the fear.)

So after one of the morning sessions, when most of the people had left, I saw an easy opportunity to ask my question. As I was gathering up my notes (and my courage), the Holy Spirit laughingly piped up, "He won't tell you."

"Excuse me?" I countered. "What do You mean: he won't tell me? He's the one that gave the word!" (Fortunately I wasn't actually saying this out loud. It was an internal conversation.)

"He won't tell you, because this isn't about a conversation with him. It's about a conversation with Me."

I sank, deflated, back into my seat. This whole process...this *journey-with-God* thing was far more challenging than I had anticipated. When I had finished feeling sorry for myself, I just packed up my bag and left for lunch. After the school, I went home to California, still wondering what the phrase meant.

My contemplations had continued with seemingly little progress for a couple of months when I experienced a wonderful provision of favor. I was a school teacher at the time, and through a series of bureaucratic miracles, I was given a fully-paid trip across the country to attend a premier education training event in Boston; a city that I had always dreamed of visiting. I was immersed in American history heaven, which was equaled only by scoring tickets to see the Red Sox play the Yankees at Fenway Park. Life was good.

On the second afternoon of the training course, a water main ruptured in the lecture hall that we were in. The entire class was moved into an impossibly small room for the remainder of the week. The only way we could all fit in the room was to sit with our chair backs touching the table behind us—meaning that if you were sitting next to the wall, the only way that you could exit was to have your entire row stand up to allow you to get out.

Late on the third day, I was in my assigned seat against the wall as I listened to a discourse on the wonders of innovative reading comprehension. I gradually realized that I was beginning to feel funny: my stomach began to flutter, and I felt a bit light-headed. Just when I thought these sensations might have something to do with combining New England clam chowder and Boston baked beans for lunch, I realized that my physical symptoms were actually a reaction to a growing, profound, Holy Spirit presence. I felt tangible waves of warm glory wrap around me and began to experience a love so magnificent that I could barely see or think. All I wanted to do was escape so that I could be alone and worship.

But I was trapped! There were thirty minutes left until the end of the session, and I had no way of getting out. I considered limbo-ing my way under the table, but legs from humans and chairs made that impossible. I had no choice. I was stuck.

For that remaining half hour, I was immersed in the love of God as I had never encountered it before. I exerted a great deal of effort to simply sit still, hoping not to draw attention to myself. After what seemed like an eternity, the class ended. I hurdled my way out of the room, dashed across the street (possibly through insane traffic) and up the stairs to my hotel room, slamming the door behind me. Finally, I was free to worship with the abandon that God's presence deserved!

And then, there was...nothing. Not a goose bump, not a shiver, and no warm anything—just four walls in the Beacon Street Holiday Inn and a lot of empty air.

I was crushed. Where had God gone? The intensity of the experience in the classroom had to mean *something*. I sat for a long time, waiting for it to return, but it didn't. Finally I decided to go to dinner, completely mystified by what had occurred.

By late the next afternoon, the memory of the experience had begun to recede. I was once again tucked in my seat by the wall, when suddenly— the Presence returned, stronger than ever! And again, for about half an hour, until the session ended for the day, I was immersed in what seemed to be the very heart of God.

Once again, when class ended, I dashed out across the street and ran for my hotel room.

And once again, with the slam of the door: nothing. Absolutely nothing.

This time, I was determined not to leave so quickly. I waited twice as long as I'd waited the day before, but with the same result. What was I missing? Was there some response to God that had eluded me? Maybe He was waiting in the hallway? A quick visit outside my room proved fruitless.

And as you may have guessed already, the next day, we repeated this cycle once again. But my response when I arrived at my room was quite different: I was mad. (Yes, I'm well aware this was not a good response. Save your letters and emails; I agree with you.) "Alright, enough! I love Your Presence. I want Your Presence in this amazing way, but why do You keep leaving?" I tossed my armload of textbooks on the ground like a petulant child. "Tell me what You're doing!"

And in an infinitely kind, internal voice, God simply answered, "Sit down." All my frustration melted away as I realized how thankful I was just to hear Him again. As soon as I was seated in the overstuffed chair in the corner of my room, the waves of love and goodness and kindness and passion began again. I felt like a found lost sheep, and I fairly wriggled with joy. Finally! I could respond! I jumped to my feet and began to worship, telling God how magnificent He was and how much I adored Him. But I was interrupted.

"Please stop doing that," He gently but firmly said. "Sit down."

I thought I certainly had heard wrong. Stop? Why? That's what worship is about! It's our way of responding to God's glory, and I had been waiting literally days to do it!

While I am well-loved, I can also be a slow learner. God would manifest His Presence, and I couldn't help but express my worship to Him—only to have Him still me again. We repeated this exchange several more times, until finally all my protests drained away.

In that place of stillness, God quoted back to me the phrase that I had been pondering for so long. *"I do not seek your adoration. I seek your blessing. Adoration is a consequence of a life beloved. It seeks to love in return. I seek to love, and love, and love. I seek to love for the sake of loving. For I am Love. And as My love is poured out and received, it comes back to Me. The more extravagantly you allow yourself to receive love, the more you will become beloved."* *

As His majesty increased in the hours that followed, I got it. He was answering my question that I'd asked months earlier. He wanted me to become a fine-tuned *receiver* of His love, not always a broadcaster. My reaction of immediately responding with worship prevented Him from lavishing the depths of His passion on me. I was tossing adoration back to Him the moment I encountered Him, but He wanted me simply to bless what He was doing so that it would go deeply into my spirit. When He answered me, He was kind enough to put me in an assigned seat by the wall in a tiny classroom in Boston, where I couldn't escape: I had to sit and take it—which was exactly what He wanted.

Excerpt from "Inheritance and Glory," by Graham Cooke, transcribed at the end of the book "Prophetic Wisdom," available at www.BrilliantBookHouse.com.

That encounter completely revolutionized my worship life. My greatest joy has been to become a great receiver, learning to receive from Him, before being a champion broadcaster, telling Him how wonderful He is. Ministering to the Lord now means investing in the time to be filled with His delight in me — to return worship to Him from His abundance, not my reactive effort. I still practice being in His presence in a deep and enduring way, but in Boston, God had set the flow in the right direction: receiver first, tuned into His frequency, overwhelmed from the fullness of His love to overflow eventually (not always immediately) back to Him.

There are still many days where my worship is boisterous, full of praise and expression, but it is not the only station on my radio receiver anymore. Hidden, at the end of the dial, is my favorite station of all: the one that plays His songs over me — where my only response is to sit, breathe deeply, and listen closely — to worship through beholding…and beholding…and beholding…until I have become the Beloved He has always seen.

Mindset #6: Fine Tuning Your Receiver

1. What is the current condition of your internal receiver? Is it quiet, or is there a lot of static from internal conversations?

2. If there is static, what is it usually from? Worry? Fear? Replaying previous conversations, or planning ahead for ones that haven't occurred yet? Condemnation?

3. What aspect of God's nature do you want to tune into most to displace this?

4. What is He doing in your life that He simply wants you to bless and receive deeply?

5. As you pursue this process, remember that God is delighted to bring you back to stillness as many times as needed. He never tires of it, because He is so happy that you are pursuing becoming a brilliant receiver of all that He wants to be for you.

MINDSET #7:
POWERFUL CHOICES

"I feel like a kid in a candy store!" is a familiar phrase. It captures the excitement and joy of unlimited choices. The concept of being surrounded with bright, colorful, tasty delights and of being a kid (which makes the unabashed adoration and consumption of sweets acceptable) is one that brings a smile to most people's faces. But having a vast array of options does not always produce a positive response, nor does it guarantee satisfaction. In fact, too many choices can easily become overwhelming.

I first encountered this concept in the 1980s with a group of foreign exchange students from the Soviet Union who had been given the chance of a lifetime to visit the United States. At that time, governmental restrictions had just begun to loosen enough to allow such opportunities, but receiving permission to travel to the U.S. was still extremely rare.

These young people did quite well with life in our small, rural town, but, once we were on the way to the big city, it was a different story. The group's itinerary included a visit to San Francisco. My fellow teachers and I scheduled a picnic lunch for the trip, deciding to stop at a supermarket on the way so that each student could choose what they personally wanted to have for lunch.

When we first entered the supermarket, the students were delighted as they walked through the produce section, picking up fruits and vegetables that they had never actually seen. Pineapples, mangos, and watermelons were all a novel experience. One young girl held up a banana, excitedly commenting, "I once had one of these!" For the first time, I began to truly understand how limited their experiences had been...and how many foods I had taken for granted.

As I was counting my blessings, our lead teacher announced to the students that it was time for them to choose a fruit to include in their lunch. The group's mood changed quickly from awe to anxiety. Making such a choice seemed like a once-in-a-lifetime opportunity, and they became very distressed. Their smiles were replaced with furrowed brows as they contemplated their decisions. They quickly began to make bargains and deals with each other to share their choices amongst the group as a whole, so that nothing was left unexplored. Finally, one young man began to cry quietly. "It's too much!" he whispered. "It's just too much."

The other teachers and I were astonished. Our Ameri-centric brains had not anticipated their reaction. We quickly shifted our plan, and had the students wait in the van with one of the instructors while the rest of us quickly finished the shopping. If their introduction to the produce section had produced such a dilemma, having them visit the deli counter (which took up an entire wall of the store) was obviously not a good idea.

We finished our shopping and drove on to the park that we'd selected for the picnic. When we arrived, we spread out the fruit, meats, bread, and cheeses that we had selected. The students cheered up immediately and dove right in. They happily tried a bit of everything, repeatedly expressing their thanks. The boisterous, adventurous teenagers we had come to know and love over the preceding two weeks returned, and we went on to have a delightful time in San Francisco.

FREEDOM MEANS CHOICES, AND CHOOSING TAKES PRACTICE

In American culture, we are champions at making multiple choices in many areas of our lives—simply because we have so many of them to make. I once tallied up fourteen brands of soap solely for hand-washing dishes. Add to that the vast array of dishwasher powders, liquids, and tablets...then throw in soap for hands and face (shower gels, cleansing creams, bars, and liquid)…and don't forget powder, liquid, & gel laundry soaps, carpet cleaners and stain removers — well, you get the idea. Every day, we are barraged with dozens of choices just in an attempt to stay clean!

But, when it comes to life with God, many of us have experienced a religious culture in which there weren't a great many choices offered, with even fewer decisions to be made. We all made the big choice: to accept Jesus as Lord and Savior. But after that, some of us entered into spiritual communities in which a lot of our options were limited. We were offered predetermined ways to read the Bible, to pray, and had set schedules of when to come to church and what to do there. I remember that it was radical if we sang two hymns at a service instead of three! So due to a limited number of opportunities to practice, our ability to make powerful choices regarding our spirituality may well have diminished over time.

As a child growing up in church, doing things the way they were supposed to be done seemed very, very important. There were gold stars for attendance, for learning the memory verse, doing the Sunday school lesson and bringing a Bible. If I forgot any of these, I had a profound sense that God was very disappointed in me. I remember the acute embarrassment I felt for little Tommy from down the street during his first visit to our church. Having never actually been to church before, he logically thought that, when the communion wafers were passed, it was snack time. So, he took the opportunity to stock up and started eating. The people around him were actually quite nice about it, but the audible gasps for the "poor heathen child" were hard to miss. Everyone knew you weren't supposed to do that!

As I cringed for little Tommy, I also remembered feeling conflicted. Would Jesus really mind if a small child didn't understand what the crackers were for? Remembering that He chose playful kids over religious propriety once before (Matthew 19:14), something inside of me knew that little Tommy's actions wouldn't have offended Him. Was communion only official if it was a particular type of bread eaten in a particular kind of ceremony? Could we do this to remember Him at any time, or could it only be on the first Sunday of the month? For my eight year-old mind, the differences between the Jesus of the Bible and the rules and regulations of religion were often very confusing.

THE GOD WHO LOVES OPTIONS

It's impossible to read the Bible without coming to realize that God adores choices. He desires a people who can think for themselves and make decisions — so much so that the Father, Son, and Holy Spirit designed a plan of salvation that was completely dependent on it! He wants an empowered family that is in relationship with Him because they passionately choose to be. Obedience and righteousness are designed to be our free-will responses of loving Christ in return for how much we've been loved (John 14:23 and 1 John 4:19). God's grace, goodness, and patience towards us are clearly defined as the motivators for our choice of repentance (Romans 2:4). We are free to continue in our own ways, but He graciously waits for us turn and go where He is going, relentlessly kind in the face of our stubbornness (Isaiah 30:18).

Salvation itself was based on a choice — the most powerful choice ever made, and Jesus was the one Who made it. When faced with the overwhelming implications of the cross before Him, He prayed, "Father, everything is possible for You. Take away this cup from Me; yet not what I will, but what You will" (Mark 14:36, Amplified Bible). The words are so familiar, but stop for a moment to think about what He was saying. Jesus was telling His Dad that, at that moment — if it's at all possible — *He doesn't want to do this.* I've always wondered how much time elapsed between His request to the Father and His choice of action. I think it was probably more than the writing reflects; but, at some point, He had to personally make a decision to go forward.

It was possible for Jesus to have chosen His will over the Father's. Thank God that He didn't...but He could have. He had a choice. And He made that eternal choice based on His love and trust of the Father and because of joy: "...looking unto Jesus, the author and finisher of our faith, *who for the joy that was set before Him* endured the cross, despising the shame, and has sat down at the right hand of the throne of God" (Hebrews 12:2, italics mine).

If the God of the universe left the decision for our salvation fully in the hands of His Son, how could we imagine doing anything less than honoring the freedom of the people He died to give that choice to?

There are, of course, truths that are absolute in Scripture. Jesus is the son of God – not figuratively, but literally. God created the heavens and the earth (not a blast from the past). These types of truths are not based on multiple choice possibilities. But how much of what we do in our daily, practical spirituality is based primarily on patterns of familiarity? Are our actions an authentic expression of life in God, or do we do things in certain ways because that's the way that it's always been done?

Traditions are not bad in and of themselves. They can be powerful encounters with thanksgiving, remembrance, and honor. But when traditions limit our creativity and freedom, then we need to ask ourselves: "Why we are doing what we are doing?" Is it from the heart of God, or is it simply the rutted paths of standard operating procedures? If the Father trusted His Son with the choice for our salvation, could it be possible that He is willing to trust Him in us (Colossians 1:27) to make excellent choices as well?

BUT WHAT IF I MAKE A MISTAKE?

"What if I make a mistake?" is a question that gripped me for years and is one that I am frequently asked about. Fear of mistakes beckons us to create a safety net of rules to prevent every conceivable mishap. But no matter how many contingency plans we design, mistakes are not a matter of "what if?" but of "when?" There's no mystery involved. We *will* miss it, make messes, and learn what not to do because we've tried and failed. Yet each of these "mistakes" can provide an authentic experience that, if perceived and walked through properly, can be part of a genuine process of maturity. If fear of failure causes us to weave safety nets out of rules, could the very nets that we design end up bringing us into captivity to performance rather than into freedom to obey out of love?

What if the real safety net for mistakes *is* love? Consider the perspective found in 1 Corinthians 13:7-8 (Amplified Version): "Love bears up under anything and everything that comes, is ever ready to believe the best of every person, its hopes are fadeless under all circumstances, and it endures everything without weakening. Love never fails, never fades out or becomes obsolete or comes to an end." Love without conditions causes us to call each other up higher; and, if messes are made, it takes responsibility to clean them up, asks for, and extends, forgiveness, and is willing to ask "What did I learn?" and "What is missing from my experience of Christ that would cause me (or others) to behave like that?"

THE SAVIOR WHO ISN'T AFRAID OF MISTAKES

Jesus was surrounded by a ministry team that made numerous mistakes and messes. He gave instruction and strong course corrections at times, but He never abandoned them based on their poor choices. My favorite story about this is found in Luke 22, when Jesus is talking to Peter about his upcoming denial. Simon Peter truly believes that he will go to prison and even die with the Lord if it's required of him. But Jesus understands Peter better than Peter understands himself. He already knows that His friend will deny Him. And what was Jesus' response to that knowledge of Peter's pending mistake? It's found in verse 31 and 32. "And the Lord said, 'Simon, Simon! Indeed, Satan has asked for you, that he may sift you as wheat. But I have prayed for you, that your faith should not fail; and when you have returned to Me, strengthen your brethren.'"

Wait! No lectures to try to convince Peter that he wasn't where he thought he was? No rules issued to keep Peter out of the fray so that it wouldn't happen? And...no intervention to prevent Satan from trying this plan? What's up with that? The enemy had a plan to destroy Peter, and Jesus knew it. Peter was about to make a huge mistake. *But Jesus didn't stop it.*

Pause with me for a moment to notice an important facet of this story. Peter is not available to Satan for whatever he wants to do to him. The enemy has to ask God if he can sift Peter — which tells us Who is really in charge. Could it be that God is not terrified of what the enemy can try to do when He already has a plan for a good outcome? "'For I know the thoughts and plans that I have for you,' says the Lord, 'thoughts and plans for welfare and peace and not for evil, to give you hope in your final outcome'" (Jeremiah 29:11, Amplified Bible).

Jesus did, however, take action. What did He do? He prayed. Jesus prayed that Peter would not be so devastated by this reality check that his faith would fail. And Jesus doesn't stop there. He goes on to graciously paint a picture for Peter of what lay on the other side of the mistake — because He knew that, once the denial occurred, it was going to be hard for Peter to believe that God's goodness and kindness was big enough to cover his epic failure. The Lord speaks confidently about how He sees His friend, restored and helping others because of what he had learned in his experience. Jesus gave Peter a hopeful vision of his future, as an anchor for him through the coming storm. Jesus didn't say "…if you return…" but "…*when* you have returned to Me…." This was a defining moment for Peter. Would he believe that the grace of God is really that amazing?

Jesus allowed the choice to occur, but He also equipped Peter with hope and interceded for him to choose well.

Luke 22:61 says that as Peter was uttering his third vehement denial of the Lord, that Jesus turned and looked at him. Can you imagine Peter's horror? I have wondered: what did he see in that look? It couldn't have been disappointment or shock, because the Lord already knew it was going to happen. So what was it? I believe that it was a look of absolute love. Scripture clearly says that repentance is provoked by goodness (Romans 2:4), not judgement. When Jesus looked at Peter, His unconditional love, combined with His intercession to the Father and His present-future statement of hope; unlocked a passageway for Peter to travel away from condemnation, into repentance, and receive the forgiveness that was already present in the heart of God. Peter still had to choose to believe and embrace the forgiveness that was on offer, but Jesus had made every provision for him to do so. It's a pattern that continues today: Jesus continues to love us as His Father loves Him (John 17:23) and intercedes for us in Heaven before God's throne of grace (Hebrews 7:25).

Being our full time intercessor is Jesus' job now and it's a major reason that He's not afraid of our mistakes. He's very good at His job.

I've often imagined Peter in later years, leading the early church. I've wondered if there were times when persecuted Christians came to him, ashamed and devastated that they had fled under the threat of imprisonment…or worse, had denied that they knew Jesus. In those days, the Bible was still being written. The story of Peter's denial of Christ was probably not widely known. Can you imagine Peter's response to a devastated believer, overwhelmed with grief and self-loathing, who'd come him to admit their failure? I wonder if his response began with the words, "I know just how you feel. Let me tell you a story...."

The very mess meant to destroy Peter became a powerful message about a Christ who prays for us continually (Hebrews 7:25). About a Savior who sympathizes with our weakness (Hebrews 4:15) and remembers that we are made of dust (Psalm 103:14). About the Friend (John 15:15) Who sees us restored and ministering to others as we have been ministered to (2 Corinthians 1:4). About the One who is able to turn the schemes of the devil into his own defeat time and time again (1 Corinthians 2:8). God captivated Peter's heart with a love that believed the best, was fadeless under all circumstances, and had never failed—just as He seeks to captivate ours in the same manner today, because He understands something very important:

A captivated heart will freely choose to follow God.

Rules and structure based on the fear of mistakes can never create an expansive atmosphere of joy and freedom. They may achieve behavioral results, but will not contribute to lasting, relational transformation. Strict religious fences can keep everyone together, but they can also lead us to a passive expectation of a point-by-point path to follow. Without step-by-step directions, both members of a community and leaders can become overwhelmed and unsure of how to begin to take responsibility for their own journey of development with God. Paralysis from fear sets in. What if we get off course? What if errors are made? Instead of building a strong relationship with God and each other, we sadly settle for a lesser realm of powerless predictability.

Time out. In all of this discussion of powerful choices, let me be very clear: *freedom* is not synonymous with a *free-for-all*. Permission granted is not the same as permissiveness. This mindset is not about irresponsibly, purposefully making poor choices because God will fix it. God is holy, and our awe of His majesty and response of personal holiness is a hallmark of growing up into all things in Christ. We are meant to make powerful choices for righteousness and obedience to God's ways, but it is the motivation behind the desire for right living that means everything to God. "If anyone loves Me, he will keep My words" (John 14:23). Jesus didn't say this as a threat, shaking His finger in our face. Instead, I hear a confident tone in His voice. "Hey guys, be at peace. You love Me, right? Okay then. You'll want to keep My words."

When we truly believe that this is the nature of God, then we lose our apprehension of stepping into the unknown and of making a wrong choice, because there is no fear in love (1 John 4:18). We are not cavalier in our behavior, but neither are we intimidated by the possibility of a mistake. It is an act of worship to trust that God's grace is truly amazing, that the wise Mind of Christ is our inheritance, and to make bold choices in following Him.

LESSONS LEARNED ON THE FRONTLINE

I hadn't considered any of this when we developed The Warrior Class, but TWC has proven to be an amazing encounter with the impact of choice and the challenges of personal responsibility in spirituality. The vision that emerged as we gave some basic definition to our dream was to create a core process with an array of options in training and practice. We wanted to value different learning styles, distinct passions, and individual personalities.

For example: while our extroverts might love our conference calls, our introverts probably wouldn't as eagerly participate. So, we welcomed our introverts into that space by offering them the option to join us on the calls as a listener only and then email us about what they heard and thought as they listened to the group conversation. We value personal passion by allowing our members to choose what order they wish to go through the materials and how long they spend with each one within our twelve month time frame for each level. Our "Member Only" website contains a vast array of resources to draw from in their process. In essence, we have created a "Tool Room" with various building supplies, coaching and options. We offer a framework with which to build from; but each member is responsible for constructing their own unique habitation with the Lord.

One of our strongest values in The Warrior Class is: this is your story and journey with God, and your responsibility to craft it primarily with Him, not only with us. We have no desire for deadlines and exams to be the motivation that keeps people going. Passion for Jesus and powerful choices that lead to joyful, purposeful actions is our goal.

CHOICES BRING FREEDOM FROM HAVING TO DO IT ALL

What we didn't anticipate, though, was the gap that would become evident between loving the concept of Joyful Intentionality and actually learning to live in it. During our first year, I remember having a phone conversation with one of our newer members. She was trying to sort out the core program from the options. After I had clearly explained it (for the third time), I realized that something else was going on. She continued to ask about the advantages to each of her choices…and the pitch of her voice got continually higher and more frantic. I began to understand what she was really struggling with, but I wanted to see if she could understand it for herself. And to her credit, she did.

"But… But… (Deep sigh.) I can't do all of this!"

There it was. She had uncovered the root of her aggravation. No matter how many times I told her that these were options, her performance mindset couldn't let go of the need to *do it all* to be successful.

It's a common upgrade that most of our members encounter and the freedom that we see as they embrace the reality of being trusted to make powerful choices is profound. I would love to take credit for the strategy, but it was pure Holy Spirit genius that guided TWC to a format in which people are required to take personal responsibility and to make independent choices as to which of our options they will avail themselves of — and then are confronted with the opportunity to choose to believe that we really mean what we say when we tell them that they're not expected to do it all. Permission granted sounds wonderful, but I know from personal experience that performance junkies are completely disoriented by it.

I've had people say, "Just tell me what to do!" because the challenge of choices made the land of checklists a seemingly more desirable place. Like the newly freed Israelites, exploring an unfamiliar landscape that required faith and trust, the allure of pre-determined programs (in Israel's case, returning to Egypt and slavery) actually seemed a better option at times. Apparently, freedom takes some getting used to!

The ability to make powerful choices comes from understanding our true identity and destiny. Otherwise, we will become overwhelmed by our limitless possibilities.

We need the Holy Spirit as our Guide if we're to have a successful expedition into the vast expanses of possibilities that comes with freedom to make powerful choices based on understanding which Kingdom assignments are ours; and which are not. If the enemy can't convince us to remain passive couch potatoes, he will flood us with every good thing to do the minute we are inspired to leave the couch! Satan hopes that we become burned out by working from the false premise that if there is a need or opportunity, and we are available, it is automatically ours to fill. Years ago, I was blessed to have wonderful mentors in prison ministry who taught me:

Never engage in ministry based on need, because the need is endless.

I was raised to value Jesus' example of working within His identity and destiny. He only did what He saw His Father doing (John 5:19). He didn't automatically do what others wanted Him to do, even when it was His own family (Mark 3:31-33). He knew His Kingdom assignment and He remained faithfully focused on it.

I first learned the value of this truth during the years that I worked with Aglow Prison Ministry, especially when there were empty spaces to be filled in the prison meeting schedule. At the time, we were covering weekly services in English and in Spanish on various yards in the two largest women's prisons in the world with a total population of 8,000 inmates. We were responsible for supplying teams for the main yards, processing yards, infirmary and for a short time, the psychiatric unit. If we didn't have a team, it meant that those inmates might not receive a time of worship, teaching, prayer and encouragement.

While I was glad to call people and ask if they were available when there was a gap in the schedule, thanks to my excellent mentoring, using the leverage of "we need you" was never an option. In the years that I was responsible for that schedule, only twice did we not have who we needed when we needed them, and both times, the services were cancelled;

once was due to fog and the other due to a power outage at the prison. It was an excellent training ground in trusting His faithfulness, rather than reacting to need and of the power of cultivating a ministry environment based on passion and choice.

The Holy Spirit works to connect us with our true identity and from that, determine what our Kingdom assignments are (and what they are not). In partnership with Him, we can accurately choose what to say "yes" to and what we can freely say "no" to. No one can, or is meant, to do it all, and we are free to release "need" as our only determining factor. If we choose wisely, then the work of the Kingdom is accomplished by a Christian community that is renewed, well-equipped, powerful and supportive of each other. We celebrate those who do the amazing things we are not called to be or do, and rejoice in the freedom from the false weight of responsibility to do it all.

CHOICES WILL CHALLENGE US...AND THAT'S OKAY

This is why our first level of development in The Warrior Class focuses on identity. We want our members to understand who God made them to be, and from that, what their own Kingdom Assignments are. We make no apologies in TWC for the conflicts that our members inevitably go through in having to learn how to work with God in choosing both the path of development and the pace that He has designed for them. Many people have never experienced that choice before, but we will not become champions or game-changers unless we develop the capacity to joyfully take personal responsibility and make powerful choices. Our fear of making a mistake is displaced by our encounters with the true nature of God's expansive permission and provision. We embrace the authentic learning of what not to do as much as we value learning through our successes.

Whenever this topic comes up, I'm often asked if we have any parameters in The Warrior Class. Of course we do! But once again, it's the foundation that they are built on that makes all the difference.

The best foundation for the work of the Kingdom is built on values and principles — not rules and regulations.

We have a high value for excellence and we encourage and equip our members to rise to it, but their response is their responsibility. We have plans and strategies for how we want to grow in the next three to five years. Our preparation in that is highly intentional, but we remain flexible in how we make the journey. We have timelines for our training, but if a Warrior is having difficulty getting there, then it's a great opportunity for a dialogue about the reasons why. Is an upgrade in intentionality or in prioritizing their passions available? Has their season shifted them into a new assignment? It's never a problem; it's a possibility to get greater clarity on their story and journey with God.

Sure, the path we've chosen can sometimes be a bit messy and unpredictable. But the experiences we've had and the stories that we've already lived through have been worth every unexpected adventure. The glory of the authentic A-ha! moments and the glimpses of what Kingdom come looks like are too amazing to miss. Yet it's the joy of watching people discover a life in God lived from passion, not only duty; of seeing the desire for righteousness rise because of God's goodness; of the wonder in the voices saying, "You mean I *really* get to choose?"—that are the priceless treasures that make all the uncertain moments worth it.

And, as far as I can tell? We're just getting started. There's a growing number of people across the Body of Christ, who dearly love God and are weary of business as usual. They are willing to venture forth with a compass and a kiss—trusting the True North of God's unchanging nature and embracing His delight and permission to explore, pioneer and map a path that future generations can follow.

We'll make a million choices on our journey, countless mistakes, and magnificent discoveries. But, like all great explorers, we'll encounter exceedingly abundant adventures in God that make it all worthwhile.

Mindset #7: Powerful Choices

1. Think about your thinking when you are faced with choices in the past. What has been your initial response?

2. Has the process of making choices been exhilarating? Intimidating? Overwhelming?

3. How would you describe your current decision making process for smaller, every day decisions?

4. Is it different than for larger ones (job change, significant financial decisions, major relationship choices, etc.)? If so, how?

5. How have you viewed yourself when presented with a situation in which it is not possible to do all that is before you?

6. Are there previous experiences that have defined decision making for you that need to be unlearned? If so, what are they?

7. What is the truth about making choices that you want to embrace instead?

8. How would this new perspective of making powerful choices impact your decision making process and how you view yourself in it?

Each chapter so far has been filled with a great many options
to explore, and you're about to enter the next section
that contains even more.

At one time, that may have seemed like a lot — but that's not true
for you anymore. You've entered the realm of Joyful Intentionality,
and your mindsets are upgrading.

Now, you (and the group of people you may be reading this book with),
are empowered by the knowledge that making powerful choices, in
partnership with the Holy Spirit, is just another joyful part of a life lived
in passionate purpose with God.

What will you want to explore first?

You have the freedom to mix and match.

You can read the next chapters in sequence
or jump straight to one that interests you.

All the choices are yours.

PART 2

BUILDING A
JOYFULLY INTENTIONAL
LIFE WITH GOD

THE TOOL ROOM

One of the keys to a Joyfully Intentional life is that words and thinking are followed by exploration and action. So, as you're reading this section of the book, picture yourself entering a tool room, filled with building materials and equipment that will allow you to construct your own brilliant relationship with God in a passionately, purposeful way.

Remember, these are not more things to do for God.
They are creative ways of being with Him.

They are *descriptive*, not prescriptive. The ideas and stories should spark your own thoughts about your relationship with God, not just give you a laundry list of activities that you need to complete. Like a true warehouse of building supplies, each builder can have the same items available but no one will use them in exactly the same way.

In the Kingdom, we are interested in building
unique dwelling places with God,
not a cookie-cutter subdivision.

The ideas in these chapters are meant to be changed and expanded. They describe ways that I and my friends have explored this life, and they are offered as a catalyst for you to investigate your own. Your chief partner is the Holy Spirit. He is a genius Architect and Contractor, helping you to draw, create, and build your own habitation with God.

Enjoy the exploration!

TOOL #1:
THE END OF JOURNAL GUILT

I used to have quite the collection of beautiful journals in which only the first few pages contained writing. Each represented another staunch resolution (often made around New Year's) that, THIS time, I would write in my journal every day. And when I failed to write one day...then several days...then weeks in a row, I would abandon the process altogether — and my refugee journal stack grew. Maybe you're a naturally gifted journaler, but I was not. I desperately wanted to be, but my pile of barely used, beautiful blank books was a testament to my repeated, failed attempts and became a constant source of condemnation.

Thankfully, I've discovered several wonderful keys that have unlocked me from my prison of Journal Guilt. And if that same remorse has held you captive too, sort through these options. You may just find a key here that brings freedom to treasure your discoveries in new and unique ways.

ANNIHILATING THE MYTHS OF JOURNAL WRITING

As with everything, our thinking determines our behavior. How we think about journaling becomes the foundation that we build upon, allowing it to successfully become a valuable part of our lives. As we clear the ground of our thoughts for that good foundation, there's several obstacles that we can annihilate, replacing them with truth that sets us free.

Myth #1: Good journalers write a certain amount every day.
Truth: There are no rules!

Who said you had to write in a journal every day? Where does it say that it has to be a certain number of words or in a particular style? There is no secret, sacred "Rule Book for Journaling." You are free to record your journey in any way that works for you.

It's the *outcome* of your journaling that needs to remain your focus: finding a way to capture and treasure your relational process with God, so that you can continue to dig deeper and mine out all the wealth He has hidden in that process for you.

As my singer/songwriter friend, Bob Book, read one of my original manuscripts for Joyful Intentionality, he said he realized that his songs and his song writing process have been his way of journaling for many years. They have become an artistic expression of his travels with God, a testament to his on-going divine conversation.

Maybe you're a picture person. You may find joy in collecting images that reflect your story with God. Take a moment to jot down a few words about each image as you collect it, enough to trigger your thoughts about what sparked a connection with that picture. And leave space to jot down future inspirations when you look at it again.

If you're a poet, your journal may look more like a collection of poetic or devotional writings. One of my friends adds a verse to a poem of his life once a year. After many years of writing just one portion each year, he's created an amazing word picture of his story and journey with God. You might paint, sculpt, quilt, or create other works of art as your form of contemplation. Consider writing a paragraph or two about the resulting imagery and how it connects to your journey.

You don't have to be a prolific writer to keep a personal, meaningful record of your process and journey. God is not grading your spelling or punctuation. Don't compare your personal writing style or length of entries to anyone else's. If just a few words describes your process well enough that you could read it years later and remember exactly what you were sharing with God at that moment? Then you have enough words.

But however you choose to record your journey —
find an enjoyable process that works for you.
It is worth it. The treasures are immense!

Our adversary is a thief who wants to steal the pieces of your process before they can become useful to you. He knows that, if you begin to collect your discoveries, and continue to reflect on them, he's in big trouble. He has a vested interest in distracting you from documenting your journey, because you can use that record as a weapon to fight him on the days you feel discouraged. When you discover a way to chronicle your process, you will have evidence of God's faithfulness quickly accessible any time the enemy wants you to forget about it! As you start reading your written testimony, especially aloud, your anxiety, discouragement, and passivity will begin to evaporate. You'll begin to make divine connections between God's faithfulness to you over the course of your journey and what you may be currently encountering. Instead of the enemy's cloud of distraction and delay, you'll see clearly what God has planned for you instead (Jeremiah 29:11).

Clarity of vision that comes from having your heart settled in the
history of God's faithfulness is one of the devil's worst nightmares.

So, embrace the freedom to record your journey in a way that is authentic for you. You will have your own unique rhythm. Follow that flow. Ask the Holy Spirit, your Helper, to show you how journaling works best for you. He doesn't have a rule book. He has creativity, permission and encouragement that He'd love to share with you.

Myth #2: Journaling is self-centered.
Truth: Your life IS important. Meditating on it with God is always a good investment.

Can you believe that someone actually told me that journaling was being self-centered? At the time, I totally agreed with them. And who was the person promoting this opinion? It was me!

I felt totally weird writing about my day and what I did. At the time, it seemed self-centered and felt wildly uncomfortable. Blah, blah, blah... me, me, me. Me writing about me? But that all changed when I discovered what God loved, adored, valued, and highly treasured…and it was me, me, me!

When I finally was able to step off the edge of the journaling cliff, I chose to write my personal journal as a dialogue with God. That was what felt authentic. It became my written conversation with Someone I loved. I began to write my worship, write the questions that I was asking Him, and write about things I was pondering. And the glorious result? When I started to write my conversation with God, He began to talk back — so I wrote that down, too.

Over time, I've found that I get a better perspective of my earth-bound thinking when I see it in writing and of His elevated perspective as I write down His replies. I can see my thoughts and ways becoming more like His, and that's encouraging. I don't try to organize this journal. I just write it as it comes. And it has grown into a wonderful record of our divine friendship, one that I treasure.

Myth #3: I'll never really use my journals, so why bother?
Truth: If you don't create them, you'll never find out, will you?

The grand variations and uses for journals that we are about to explore will blow this myth out of the water. (Not to mention that this entire book was birthed out of thoughts, conversations, and content from at least four of my different journals. Oh yeah…you'll use them!)

BECOMING A DOT COLLECTOR

Before we talk about ways to keep more traditional journals, let's explore some creative variations. I like to call these variations "Dot Collecting." My logical brain used to demand that I wait to write until I could see the entire picture or felt that I had a grasp of what God was doing. For me, this meant that, by the time the pieces began to fall into place and the picture began to take shape, I had lost a bunch of the pieces — simply because I'd forgotten them!

One day, I decided to stop fulfilling the needs of my brain and to embrace the desires of my heart. I was sad to realize that I was continually losing so many potential treasures, and it finally dawned on me that I was following another set of imaginary rules that God didn't have. So, I began keeping a shoe box on my desk—first in my classroom when I was a school teacher, and now in my office at home. In it, you'll find scraps of paper, Post-Its, and often place mats or napkins from restaurants. These are my dots—random thoughts, ideas, and A-ha! moments that have occurred to me throughout the day and were quickly jotted down on whatever was handy.

Since my box is not always with me, I travel with a little note pad. I also keep one on the nightstand by my bed for those 2:00 a.m. genius moments. When I return home from a trip, I tear out the pages I've written on my travel note pad and put them in my box. I do the same thing every once in a while with one from the nightstand.

About once a month, I clear off my desk (usually with a bulldozer). I turn on my favorite music, spread out all my little pieces of paper...and the fun begins!

When I discovered that my role in this game was to be the Dot Collector—and that the Holy Spirit's job was to be the Dot *Connector*—I could relax and enjoy the process. I no longer had to figure out the big picture in advance. I could simply follow Him from one dot to the next to see if there was a correlation.

Remember those Dot-to-Dot pictures you did as a child? The simple ones were easy to guess, even before you started drawing the lines. But the challenging ones just seemed to be a giant mess. What picture could possibly be there? You couldn't tell until you began to follow the numbers and connect the dots. Little by little, an image emerged. Often it took time and the end result was surprising, but it was a delightful process. Once you'd connected all the dots in the right order, then you had a picture that you could color in.

As a Dot Collector, I've learned that sometimes I may be able to see an obvious message that quickly becomes clearer as the Holy Spirit and I sort through the papers in my box. Other times, there doesn't seem to be any rhyme or reason to the dots. When that happens, I just pile those papers back into the box. I don't need to force the connections, because that's not my job. The Holy Spirit is well able to show the connections to me when I need to see them, and I trust Him to do that. There's no pressure on me to figure out if I have all the pieces yet or not, and there's no need to rush the process. Nothing would be sillier than to try to connect five dots into a picture when the actual picture won't become evident until I have twenty of them!

Some people I know stick their dots or notes in a folder or in a drawer. Others have a "Random" notebook for disconnected thoughts. You may think of something even more brilliant. No matter how you explore this concept, become a Joyfully Intentional Dot Collector. You'll be amazed at the connections you make with the Dot Connector and the pictures that result that you didn't even imagine were possible.

CREATIVE JOURNAL MANAGEMENT

When I first came to work with Graham, I already had my conversational journal with God as a part of my relationship with Him. I also had a notebook in which I kept key prophetic words. But as we talked, I could tell that he had *a lot* of journals. One day, I asked him why. What he shared about how he organized them has saved and expanded my journaling life. So most of what follows are his genius ideas and my creative ways of implementing them.

1. Have different journals for different topics.

Having different journals for different topics brings focus when you're Dot Connecting with the Holy Spirit, and it is a huge help in knowing which journal to look in when you're searching for an idea you want to use. I probably have twelve different journals at this point. Some of them are books that I write in; others are on my computer. (Even though I regularly backup my computer, I still print out copies about once a month and put them in a notebook.)

I have a journal for The Warrior Class and another for my conversations with Graham. My "Curious George" journal contains all the questions that I'm currently pursuing with God. I have an Inheritance Word journal (with sections for notes on the key Scriptures for my life) and a separate notebook for other prophetic words I've been given. I have a journal for relationships with family and friends and the crafted prayers that I am praying for them. Instead of the old mental checklists that used to assess my growth, I now have a book of my "Evidences of Transformation." Every few months, I pull it out and take time to consider what has been transformed in my perceptions, thinking, language, and actions. My Evidences journal is also where I have notes about what areas of my life God is currently upgrading in regards to my identity and what aspect of His nature He is revealing in the process. I have a Warrior Journal in which I record the battles I encounter, the challenges I face, and God's strategies for overcoming. And I continue to record my conversations with God in another journal.

I know it sounds like a lot, but it doesn't feel that way at all. I don't write in all of them all of the time. I view them more as a library that I can read from or add to as needed. It makes my processing and sorting so much easier. Many of my journals have a pocket in the front where I can put my Dot Connecting papers, which I've found to be really helpful. If I don't have time to write extensively, but I do want to clean out my Dot Box, I do an initial sort of my notes and put them in the pockets of the journals that I'll be writing in later.

2. Create a Table of Contents.

When you begin a new journal, leave the first four or five pages blank. Then number the remaining pages in your book. (I usually do only the even numbers to save time.) These first, blank pages will become your Table of Contents, and you can fill it in as you go.

Every time you finish writing something in your journal, give it a title. Then write the title in the Table of Contents, along with its corresponding page number. That way, you'll know just where to find it when you need it.

3. Look for themes.

After you've been writing in your journal for a while, take the time to review it. Begin to see if several of your titles are connected. When you see a connection, reread those entries as one piece, to begin to see what emerges when those thoughts are grouped together. Mark the similar titles with a colored pen or pencil in the Table of Contents to remind you to continue to explore the connections they create.

This is how a great many of my talks are created. I recently put together a teaching on "Being Accepted in the Beloved" for an "Always in His Presence" conference. The journey of knowing that I am accepted by God for who I am (not what I do) has been a continuing·one. I had previously underlined entries with this theme in a couple of different journals. When I put them all together, there was a brilliant teaching that emerged, including a photograph that I use at the end of the talk, which I had pasted in to one of the pages.

Quality teaching that brings actual transformation with lasting impact can only be created over time. It can never come just from what we know about, but from a personal encounter with God. We have to behold and behold and behold who God is in that truth until we have become it ourselves. Our journals are a way of beholding; of finding different facets of truth that are authentic to our journey. When we write, teach or share from that place, there will be a multi-layer impact for the listeners that can be revisited again and again. Finding the common themes in your entries can help you explore and communicate the truths you discover in a deeper and more lasting way.

4. Read your journals for meditation and prayer.

Meditation is simply defined as "thinking deeply about something." As Christians, our goal isn't to empty our minds but rather to fill them up with God's thoughts. If I'm about to spend time in prayer about The Warrior Class, I'll often pull out my TWC journal and read it again. It contains a mix of strategies and random thoughts, challenges and victories, praise and questions. Just looking through its pages stirs up a deep sense of wonder and thanksgiving in me for God's faithfulness on this journey.

For whatever journal I choose, when I read the questions I've had and then continue on to read how God has wonderfully answered them, my faith rises to know that whatever I may currently face is in the hands of the same faithful God who walked me through those previous days of questions and answers. Sometimes, I even find the answers to my prayers already written!

Reading through a journal is a wonderful way to retrace the steps of your journey with God and to thank Him for each twist and turn. And when you pray from that unique place of remembrance and thankfulness, you'll find yourself praying from an entirely different, elevated perspective than you might have entered your intercession with.

5. Review Your Journals to Discover Your Provision

Your provision for today is often hidden in your journal entries from months ago (sometimes years ago). If you're not hearing from God on a matter, it could be because He's already answered you! It's been amazing to see how often the strategies and revelations I need for today have already been recorded in what I've written in the past.

I recently pulled out a binder of old emails written between myself and the leader of the previous prayer network in our ministry. In them, there's an email I wrote that included a description of a community of prayer and development that contains many elements of The Warrior Class—two years before Graham and I ever discussed it! I'd forgotten that I had this email, and I was fortunate that these particular ideas had stayed with me. (At the time, the ideas didn't seem to go anywhere, so they could have easily been lost.) You can be sure that I tucked this email safely into my Warrior Journal for future reference—to remind me that, when I seem unsure about how God's plan will develop, He has already been faithful to cultivate the dreams of where we are going tomorrow in the thoughts of today.

Reviewing my journals also keeps me from having to re-learn the same lesson again and again. I've found that there is an acceleration in growth, process, and maturity that comes from reviewing what I've already encountered on my journey and applying it to my current challenges.

Thanks to some brilliant teaching, I've learned that revelation doesn't come to us in an orderly fashion. We get bits and pieces here and there. Though our brains aren't made to receive revelation (that's a job for our spirit), they can be really helpful in organizing it if we can find a way to record what the Spirit is saying to us and keep the pieces until the picture becomes clearer.

REFLECTIONS ON THE VALUE OF JOURNALING

Whenever I consider the value of keeping a record of my journey, I remember Zebulon Pike. Zebulon Pike was a very early Western explorer. He was the first American citizen to see many remarkable places in what would eventually become the United States. However, few folks know who he was or what he explored. But say the names of Lewis and Clark, and you'll find many people who know them well. Why is that?

After all, just like Lewis and Clark, Zebulon Pike was also sent by Thomas Jefferson to explore the West (the southern part of the Louisiana Territory and the headwaters of the Red River, where he found the mountain that bears his name—Pike's Peak). In fact, Pike and his band of men set out on his mission of exploration just a few months after Merriweather Lewis, William Clark, and their legendary Corps of Discovery.

The difference? Lewis, Clark, and each of their officers kept a detailed record. Pike and his men did not. The Corps of Discovery meticulously wrote about what they saw, where they saw it, and about their personal thoughts throughout their travels. They gathered specimens and drew pictures. And on the occasions when one of them did not enter observations or impressions of the day in his journal, another man did in his, so nothing was lost. The resulting communal record is far more multi-dimensional than a single person would (or could) have created. Of the five supplies that the expedition never ran out of, three of them were pen, ink, and paper. (The other two were powder and lead.)

I am, at my very core, an explorer of the Kingdom and blessed to be part of a growing company of people who continually want to know what's possible on Earth before we get to Heaven. We are, and are becoming, a passion-driven community who desires to explore places of deep relationship, worship, revelation, and creativity with God that are off the map. But, like all true pioneers, it's not just about our individual travels; it's about embarking on a journey that leaves a path for others to follow—to go first into an undiscovered country, explore the possibilities, and create a map that opens it for anyone else who wants to go, too.

We dream of being entrusted with the treasures of the Kingdom, and we share a desire to understand God's wisdom and His mysteries. When the Spirit is roaming about, looking for a place to deposit and invest amazing revelation that will give Him a good return, I'm determined to be a be prime target. It would give me the greatest joy to think that the Father would say to the Holy Spirit: "Give it to Al. She'll keep it and cultivate it so that it will grow exponentially, impact many, and make Me look glorious in the process."

TOOL #2:
PROCESSING YOUR INHERITANCE WORDS

The first time I ever heard Graham Cooke speak in person, he mentioned Inheritance Words. I had no clue what he was talking about. But as I listened to him describe them that night, they sounded so wonderful:

"God loves to open up Scripture and choose the passage that He wants you to live in. How many of us have had those moments when Scripture has jumped off the page and wrapped itself around our hearts? Your spirit jumps, your heart pounds, and you know that God's talking to you. He wasn't giving you a passage to memorize or study (although you could do that and it would be okay). But it's something more than that. He was giving you a promise for your life: an Inheritance Word!

"When God gives you a passage of scripture like this, what He's saying is, 'Everything in this passage belongs to you. You need to stay in it until you find everything I want to give to you out of it. Every experience, every encounter in that passage is meant for you to have as well. Every promise in that passage now belongs to you. Everything I do in power in those verses, I will do for you.' It's your Inheritance Word.

"In Luke 4:18-19, Jesus walks into His hometown church and takes the scroll from the attendant. Normally, they read in sequence — so that each week they start with where they left off last. The Bible says, 'He found the place….' The Savior read out of sequence in church! He begins to read Isaiah 61, 'The Spirit of the sovereign Lord has anointed Me….' What's He doing? He's reading His

Inheritance Word. He is saying, 'This is who I Am. All these things, I can do because I'm anointed to do them. This is My inheritance Word. It belongs to Me, and I am going to become it. I am going to be the living embodiment of it.'

"So, what Inheritance Words do you have? You need to look at that word like you would study prophecy. Everything in that word is yours. If there is a person mentioned in there, you can have the same identity and the same relationship with God as they did. When God gave me Numbers 13 & 14, He said, 'I've called you to be a Caleb. I want you to swim against the tide. I want you to be a man of a different spirit. I want you to see things that can't be seen and relish the fight. You will love the presence of a giant, because you know I'll always be bigger.'

"If you haven't had a Scripture like that given to you, come up here and let's pray for one right now!"

I didn't have to be asked twice. I joined a small group of people who walked to the front of the room, and Graham began to pray.

"In the Name of Jesus, I declare to you: you are now going to attract dreams, visions, prophecy, and Scripture. God is going to connect with you! God will speak to you! He will come to you and envision you with dreams and visions. The Word of God is going to come alive to you! God is going to release Scripture into your life…and when He does, He's going to be excited, saying 'THIS is who you are! Everything in this now belongs to you! In this promise, you can learn to be in alignment with Me.' We declare it in the Name of Jesus, for the sake of your role and your place in His Kingdom. In Jesus' Name."

I also remember the last thing he said before we left that night:

"It's not about you trying to get something. It's about you just being peaceful and receiving it. It's going to come. You can't stop it."

I returned to my seat to gather my things. I walked out of the sanctuary and stood in the foyer, waiting…not for my Inheritance Word, but for someone to invite me to spend the night at their house.

You see, I had driven several hours to get to the conference. A friend had given me two of Graham's teachings several months before, and they had been my lifeline. It had been a difficult week, one in which an avalanche of accusations and ministry pressures had left me spinning. Late in the week, I somehow discovered Graham would be speaking within driving distance that weekend, so Friday afternoon I jumped in my car and began driving. It was such a sudden decision that I forgot to pack an overnight case. But on the drive over, I felt God say very distinctly, "Someone will ask you to stay at their house tonight. You won't need a hotel."

So, there I was…standing in the church foyer, waiting for someone to come and invite me to their home. But no one did.

I began to feel uncomfortable after a while and wondered if I had really heard God correctly. It had *seemed* like a simple statement, but maybe there was more to it? The longer I thought about it logically, the faster my faith began to drain away. I decided I must have gotten it wrong, and I began a very slow walk to my car. Maybe a heavenly light beam would suddenly highlight me to someone if I just gave it enough time!

But no beams shone down, and I finally arrived at my car with a deep sigh. I had obviously been mistaken about what God had said. So I drove to a nearby hotel that was just a few blocks from the church — only to be informed that not only were they sold out, but so was every hotel and motel on the I-80 corridor for 50 miles. It was graduation weekend!

This left me with few options as I started walking back across the hotel parking lot. When I was about ten feet from my car, a familiar Voice behind me said with a smile, "Sweetheart, we aren't going to get very far if you don't follow simple directions. Go back to the church."

So, back to the church we went.

By now, the parking lot was dark and almost empty. A few folks were meandering out and locking the doors behind them. I didn't really want to announce that one of them was supposed to take me home, so I artfully rolled down my car window as I slowed to a stop and asked, "Do one of you happen to know a place that I could stay tonight?" I thought this was pretty creative: I wasn't specifically asking for a hotel recommendation, but I also wasn't rudely inviting myself to their home. One lady began to give me directions to where I had just been, and I explained the graduation situation. She continued to list other hotels without showing much comprehension of what I had just said.

Another woman joined the conversation. "Are you alone?" she asked, as she glanced inside my car (possibly for weapons or something suspicious...not that I blame her). As calmly as I could, I replied that I was by myself. "Why don't you come to my house then?" She went on to explain that her son was away for the weekend, and I could stay in his room—but I didn't really hear any of that. All I knew was that I had a place to sleep without having to make a complete idiot of myself. (I was going to look strange enough once I had no suitcase to explain.)

That night, after my kind hostess had said good night to her odd house guest, I remembered the Holy Spirit's voice as I left the hotel. It was so distinctly behind me. I began to think: wasn't there a verse about hearing God's voice behind you, and that He would say that this was the way to walk in? Where was that? I grabbed my Bible and began to search.

I found it in Isaiah 30. The minute my eyes fell on the passage, it was like the words took on a life of their own! The verse about hearing God's voice was actually at the end of what would become my first Inheritance Scripture. And as I went on to read the chapter, it became clearly evident where my Inheritance Word began and finished.

It started in verse 15: "In returning and rest you shall be saved. In quietness and confidence will be your strength." Then it went on to describe someone who didn't quite cooperate with that process and to describe God's response to them—which hit me like a ton of grace-filled bricks: "But I waited for you, that I might be gracious" (Isaiah 30:18).

There was a promise of the emergence of teachers in my life (verse 20) and then it ended with the wonderful words I had encountered earlier: "You will hear a voice behind you, when you turn to the left or to the right, saying, 'This is the way, walk in it.' " (Isaiah 30:21).

That took place in May of 2004. I have lived in, mined out, re-written, and explored that word for over a decade...yet I still feel as if I've just scratched the surface. Confidence in who God is for me continues to grow every time He stands in my gaps, filling them with who He is: Wisdom, Truth, and Love. He has whispered these verses in my ear when I wanted to rush forward too quickly, and He has comforted me with them when I did. They have been my safe haven and steady compass in a reinvented life that has no maps.

And at times when I have backed away from going forward, I continuously encounter God's loving nature—finding that He's waiting for me, so that He can be gracious, just as He promised. He's captivated my heart with His desire to see me advance, and He's motivated me with kindness and patience. And when I forget to respond this way to others, it is remembering how He and His friends have walked with me in grace and gentleness that breaks my heart and leads to easy repentance.

As I've grown in Him, He does not hold my hand, giving constant instructions for every step. I now understand more than ever that His answer is "Yes!" and permission really is granted for me to explore. If I get off course, He is well able to step in and show me a more excellent way. From that night in the hotel parking lot until now, the Voice behind me has been ever faithful to keep me pointed in the right direction. Sometimes He speaks directly, sometimes through His Word, sometimes through the voice of friends—but He has no difficulty making Himself heard when I am heading to the right or to the left of His best for me.

I have not studied Isaiah 30 as much as I have *encountered* and continue to become it.

The traits of verse 15 are not natural to my personality, but they are to His. I haven't tried to academically learn more about rest and quiet. Instead, I've discovered more and more of Who the Prince of Peace is to me, how He sees me, and I now reflect more of that image than I used to...though not as much as I eventually will.

He has orchestrated my circumstances so that I would have the opportunity to learn joyful dependency and trust in His unchanging nature. He detoxed me from the praise of men as a food-source for my soul. Now, the affirmation of my many friends and loved ones are a delight in my life, not a foundation for my self-esteem.

And, during the times when I was in the midst of a growth opportunity (and completely unclear as to what was really going on), my Inheritance

Word from Isaiah 30 would remind me that what I was experiencing was not warfare; it was training. I would sit with Him, and He would unfold which part of the word I was becoming at that point. My job was just to cooperate with His Word and His promises. I have always had a Helper and a Teacher in the Holy Spirit.

TREASURES FROM THE PAST

You may find that you already have Inheritance Words. Sometimes we have passages of scripture that have been life verses or that have been a deep well of encouragement that got us through a challenging time. When I first began to consider my Isaiah 30 Inheritance Word, I wondered if I had other Inheritance Words that I hadn't recognized with this mindset. In the weeks that followed, I realized that there were two: Joshua 1:9 and Isaiah 61:1-7.

When I was eight years old, I was terrified of almost everything. So my mother got me a little devotional with Joan Walsh Anglund pictures in it and one scripture on each page. She highlighted the page with Joshua 1:9 "Only be strong and very courageous, for the Lord thy God is with thee, whithersoever thou goest." I loved that little book and I would read all of the scriptures, waiting to get to *my* page. I adored saying the word "whithersoever" as a small child and would repeat it again and again. But as the years passed and my journey out of a fear-based life contin-ued, I realized how central that verse had been to me. I discovered that I was indeed a Joshua, a warrior who had developed over time, who lived to be in the presence of the Lord. I had often struggled with courage and confidence, but like Joshua, the Lord had been gracious to repeat His encouragement many times. And it had been birthed in my spirit with that verse at the age of eight.

When I was twenty-three years old, I was working in Belgium, writing letters to my soon-to-be husband back in the U.S. I had written to him that a house mate had given me the beginning verses of Isaiah 61 as a life scripture, only to find out that he had just been given Isaiah 60 in a similar way! Isaiah 61 is my foundation in the prophetic, the passion of my life: to give beauty for ashes, the oil of joy instead of mourning and to clothe people with garments of praise in exchange for heavy hearts weighed down with legalism and fear. Of course at the time, I didn't realize that it would mean that I would have times of ashes, mourning and deep sorrow...but when those times came, Isaiah 61 was an anchor to my soul like none other. It has faithfully led me to the divine exchange God always had on offer of beauty, joy and praise.

GETTING THE MOST FROM YOUR INHERITANCE WORDS

So, how can each of us discover the greatest treasure from our Inheritance Words? Without intentionality, Inheritance Words can join the ranks of other forms of God's expressions that we may have gathered — only to put on a pretty shelf and never become a living part of our lives. But, as He once reminded me, "They aren't to be collected like baseball cards. Please use them."

Here are some ways that you can mine these priceless treasures. Many of the ways will also be useful in processing your prophetic words. Both your Inheritance Words and your prophetic words are expressions from His heart to yours.

1. Get a journal just for this word.

You'll be collecting dots and bits of revelation. With a journal, you'll have a place prepared to keep them. Use the processes covered in the journaling section (Toolbox #1) to keep a record of your discoveries.

2. Ask questions for your Inheritance Scriptures.

What are the key words? Investigate their meaning in Scripture and in the original language (Hebrew or Greek if it is a verse).

Are there words or concepts that are repeated several times? Those carry more weight.

What is the primary focus of the Inheritance Word? Try giving it a title.

Write a character description of the person you see described in this Word. Does that describe you now? If there is a gap, what kind of development will you need to become what your word describes?

Study connected Scriptures in several different versions of the Bible. Do you see expanded meanings for your life?

3. For Inheritance Words, write your own version.

Drawing from your research of word meanings (and using examples that you have a personal connection with), write the passage in a personalized version.

For example: In my Psalm 139 Inheritance Word, verse 5 says, "You have hedged me behind and before, and laid Your hand upon me."

My personalized version of verse 5 ends with "…You have confidently placed your enormous hand of blessing on my head." The personalization comes out of my experience on a precious night of ministry during a time of deep struggle in my life. When the well-known minister stood before me to pray, I remember the feel of his hand on my head. He was a very big man, and the hand felt more like a giant paw. I can still feel the strong confidence that was in that hand and the kindness that resonated in his voice. The end of verse 5 seems like a simple statement; but for me, the comfort, assurance, and confidence that God has me covered is reflected simply by adding the word "enormous" that evokes that particular memory.

4. Explore creative expressions.

You may see a picture on a card or in a magazine that captures the identity that you see reflected in your overall word, or there may be one line of it that is totally captured by an image that you find. I keep mine posted on a board in my office and change them frequently. I have picture books that I created of photographs that express Psalm 139 and Isaiah 61 (two of my key Inheritance Words). The notebooks I have for my prophetic words have pictures on the covers that reflect the contents inside.

If you're a painter: paint! If you are a wood-carver: carve! And if you don't think of yourself as a particularly creative person, ask a friend who is and see if they might be able to create something for you. Or enjoy asking the Holy Spirit if there is a way to express and treasure this word in a way you have not previously explored. You may be more creative than you realize.

Inheritance Words are treasures, waiting to be mined. No one would consider following a treasure map just to discover where the "X" that marks the spot is, and then walk away! When we discover our Inheritance Words, we want to excavate them and continue to explore the depths of the riches they contain.

Make that an enJOYable process.

TOOL #3:
"BUT I DON'T HAVE A PROPHETIC WORD!"

"But I don't *have* a prophetic word!" I've lost count of the number of times I've heard this statement — usually following a message about using your prophetic words to better understand your persona or your identity, or after a teaching on pulling your future words of destiny into today. I understand how people can feel this way.

In many circles, official prophecy only takes the form of being called out from a crowd by a recognized prophet, having a prophetic appointment with a team, or in some way receiving a statement that is preceded with, "Thus saith the Lord…." It's made me sad to watch people walk away after teachings that provide great opportunities to interact with God, disappointed because they think they don't have access to prophetic ministry.

Good news! Our creative God has endless ways of communicating what He's thinking and feeling. Since His precious thoughts towards us "…outnumber the sands of the sea…" (Psalm 139:17-18), what fun would it be for Him to always communicate in the same, repetitive way? His variety builds our sensitivity. If every word that God had for us came written out in neon lights, we wouldn't need much discernment or have a need to develop our dependency on the Holy Spirit. Personally, I think He delights in creating opportunities for us to seek and keep on seeking, with a promise that we will find (Matthew 7:7). Kids play hide and seek for a reason: it's fun.

So, how might God be communicating to you in ways that you've not recognized? Where are the prophetic words in your life hiding—words that can accelerate your journey and give more definition to your destiny? Let's look at some possibilities.

CORPORATE PROPHETIC WORDS

The first time I heard a corporate prophetic word was at Graham Cooke's 2005 conference, *Seasoned in the Prophetic*. The last session of the conference included a 45-minute prophetic word on "Latitude and Indulgence." I still vividly remember that session: I was soaking it all in, laying on the carpeted floor with my eyes closed, feeling like I'd walked through a Narnian wardrobe as Graham prophesied the vast territory of God's permission and His nature of abundance.

And as the word was drawing to a close, I felt as if I was surfacing after a deep dive in the ocean: the weight of God's glory was so tangibly heavy that it seemed difficult to have a reasonable thought. I was totally captivated by the presence of God. I felt a slight sense of sadness because it was all going to be over soon. It never occurred to me that this corporate experience could actually be a beginning, not an ending.

Graham closed the session and the conference with this admonition:

"Take hold of everything you've received. Don't ever be passive again. Jesus deserves your focus and your best intentions. This whole weekend has been about God saying, 'Yes!' — and the importance of you saying 'Yes!' back.

"You've taken ground internally. Don't go back. Go further forward. He's your Father, so you can go farther. A place has opened up in front of you these last few days. This is Sacred Space, which is on the inside of you — so you're taking it with you. Go through every message. Replay the evening CDs, do the exercises, embrace the prophetic words and continue in them so that you may grow and be established...."

After he expressed his thanks to the worship team and the conference staff, those in attendance broke out in grateful applause as thanks towards Graham. But he talked over the applause until it stopped, wanting to give us one last thought:

"There's only one way you can thank me, and that is by staying at the level you've just moved into. But, if you really want to thank me? Explore."

I was so grateful for all I had just encountered that my immediate thought was, "I am going to do that! I'm going to establish and explore."

It wasn't complicated. I just followed the instructions. I listened again to the teachings and did the exercises, but it was the prophetic word of "Latitude and Indulgence" that became my main focus of exploration.

Using the conference recording, I transcribed the word. Then I used different colors to highlight the promises, conditions, and descriptions in the transcribed prophecy that painted a portrait of the attributes of someone who was fully living in the reality that the prophecy described. (Yes, this is what weirdly passes for fun when you love process.) I had conversations with the Lord about the attributes—about the ones that I could already see in my life, and about the ones that didn't seem evident at all (yet). I made separate lists of just the promises, and I read them aloud. If there were sections of the word that I didn't quite understand, I asked the Lord questions. Even though transcripts and color-coding were involved, it wasn't about studying the word so much as it was about having an on-going conversation with the Lord about what the word meant for my life and journey.

It was a year or so after that conference that I heard another teaching by Graham in which he referred to pulling your future into today by actively processing and working with your prophetic words.

"But…I don't have a prophetic word!" I exclaimed to the Lord.

"Yes, you do," He answered.

Now, for some ridiculous reason, I still occasionally have days where I tend to think that the Lord is wrong and I'm right. I don't know why this mindset persists, but it sometimes surfaces. And that was one of those days.

We had several more rounds of "No, I don't!" and "Yes, you do!" before I remembered just Who I was having a conversation with. When I did, I finally asked the question that He'd graciously waited for me to ask:

"Where's the word that I have?"

"It's your 'Latitude and Indulgence' notebook."

I was shocked. I'd heard and studied the corporate word as a prophetic word—not my prophetic word.

My mindset totally shifted (which, of course, had been His goal all along). God knew that once the corporate word became personal to me, the impact that it had on my life would be exponential. I began to study my notes with an entirely different perspective. And, over time, as I thought deeply about what God was saying in "Latitude and Indulgence," what began as "a word" became "my word."

Yes, there were certainly lots of people in the room with me during that session who also heard the word (I wasn't singled out from the platform for a "Thus saith the Lord..." moment), and the word certainly had a corporate application for that particular community of believers. But the investigation of the promises, the conversations that I continued to have with God about what the word meant for me, and the prayers that resulted were a very personal interaction between myself and God. So many truths and phrases from that word became exceptionally personal for me because of what I experienced as God and I explored it together.

In case I'd missed His point, God decided to underscore the value of a corporate word at the next conference I attended. I'd made an appointment with a prophetic ministry team. I eagerly awaited receiving my first "real" prophetic word—only to have every word that was given to me by the team somehow refer back to the new corporate prophetic word that he had given the night before ("Favor As You've Never Heard It Before"). One person prophesied: "That word is all about your life. You will spend this next season living and becoming that word." My bright, shiny, much-anticipated "personal" prophetic word was all about exploring another corporate one!

My first thought?

"Guess I'll need another notebook."

Every corporate body is comprised of individuals. That's why corporate prophetic words can have both a corporate and an individual application. In addition to the implications for the community as a whole, the word also holds an inheritance for every person that hears it, because it is based on Kingdom truth.

Corporate words are not "runner up" words to tide you over until you get "real" ones. Much of personal prophetic ministry is spontaneous, which is fine and can be a great blessing. But corporate words are more crafted and intentional. They have been pondered with the Lord for weeks, months, or even years before being intentionally and specifically delivered by a prophetic minister to a particular community. They are characterized by their amazing depth, height, and breadth to be explored, and the possibilities that they contain to be discovered when you interact with the Holy Spirit (who will personalize them just for you) are stunning.

PROPHETIC CONVERSATIONS

When I started to work with my current community of friends in Brilliant Perspectives, other people began ask me what it was like have access to so many personal prophetic words. (They'd try to be subtle about how they asked, but that was always the essence of their probing questions.) My response was, "What words?" I was puzzled by their fascination.

Then it finally dawned on me: when you work with and encounter a lot of prophetic people, other folks can think that you personally get loads of prophetic words. But that's not the case at all—at least, not in the way people think about "official" kinds of prophecy. My friends and I don't proclaim prophecies over each other every time one of us walks through the door. Absurdly enough, I think this is what some people imagine!

What *is* delightful is the natural prophetic conversations that we often find ourselves in: spontaneous dialogues in which we explore who we are and are becoming, both individually and corporately. We discuss what's possible in all aspects of life, both locally and around the world. I love how we see a bigger picture together than we can see by ourselves. We often articulate how we view each other, providing an elevated perspective that can often be hard for us to see on our own. Most importantly, we remind each other who we *really* are when our true persona seems unclear. All of this usually occurs naturally and spontaneously, weaving in and out of everyday conversations held at a dinner table, on the phone, or on a drive to pick up something from a store.

Prophetic conversations are subtle. They can be hidden among a few sentences in a laughter-filled exchange or in a comment that is muttered softly. Sometimes, the only clue that you're hearing a statement that's coming from the Spirit is the impact that it makes on you as you listen. Sensitivity and dependency on the Lord is required to not miss them. These dialogues require following the flow of what God is saying, even though everyone involved may not immediately realize that a prophetic river has opened up in the conversation.

"Prophetic dialoguers" are skilled at making a deposit into your life while pick-pocketing it at the same time. They'll steal that lesser thought that you have about yourself when you're not looking and deposit a more glorious one for you to have instead. I've listened as someone (or myself) made a self-deprecating joke and had prophetic friends artfully express the opposite, positive character they see instead. It's done light-heartedly, but the statement of true identity leaves the jokester seeing themselves more as God sees them. Any wound that caused their lesser thinking ends up with healing balm on it...if you can hear and receive the encouragement. And if you can't? Good prophetic dialoguers are patient; content to find many creative ways to speak the Truth to you until you believe it for yourself.

When you pay attention and pull God's perspectives out of these casual, future-focused exchanges that you may have with your friends, you'll find that you have some quality prophetic deposits in your life to explore and develop.

PROPHETIC SONGS

God's voice isn't always in the spoken word. A beautiful expression of His heart towards us also comes in prophetic songs. These are not songs about God. These are songs *from* Him. I have often discovered the next piece of my destiny, the comfort I need, or wisdom for my journey through listening to prophetic songs.

For years, my friend Bob Book has written and sung amazing thoughts from the heart of the Father. In his years of creating a worship atmosphere for gatherings in our community, he has consistently opened a place for Heaven and Earth to meet. His season of "Sacred Space" sessions profoundly expanded my worship perspective and remain some of my most treasured worship experiences.

For this section of the book, I asked Bob to describe a prophetic song — how it is created and how it can impact our lives as a true prophetic word.

"As I understand Biblical prophecy: in its simplest terms, it is a message for someone, from God, delivered by someone else on His behalf. This someone else (the prophet) is typically human — although on one occasion it appears a donkey delivered such a message to a human Prophet (See Numbers 22:21-35).

When God speaks, things happen! Genesis 1 is a great example of the creative power released when God speaks. Even a cursory examination of prophecy in the Bible would lead me to conclude that prophetic messages from God release creative power in the lives and situations of those who receive them. Paul says in 1 Timothy 4:14 (for example) that Timothy's ministry gift was given to him through a prophetic message.

Songs are powerful. They can stir and motivate us in ways as few other things can. When combined with the creative power contained in a prophetic message, prophetic songs not only stir and motivate us but release an enabling anointing that empowers us to be who God says we are and do what God says we can do.

This prophetic song, then, is written in first person, as God singing directly to the listener.

<u>STRONG</u>

I know you're anxious about tomorrow,
it's like a monkey on the back of your mind.
You're losing sleep, losing perspective.
You feel so weak, but you know it's plain to Me.

Chorus:

You're strong.

You are courageous.

The heart of the lion beats inside of you.

You're strong.

You are contagious.

Because I am the Superhero, living inside of you.

I know you worry about the future.

I see the fear just gnawing at you.

Lift up your head, turn My direction.

Look through the smoke and mirrors

and you'll see it's really true.

Who is this song for? You! If you have opened your life to Jesus, Holy Spirit resides in you — so this is how God sees you: STRONG! It is critical to God that you see yourself this way. This is what's true about you, so it's important that your self image matches God's image of you. Listening to this song is like seeing yourself in Heaven's mirror. This is the true you!

I was inspired to write this song by the account of Gideon found in Judges 6. The Angel of the Lord finds Gideon in a winepress, threshing wheat. This is clearly not the usual use for a winepress, but Gideon is doing his best to keep himself and the bit of sustenance he can seek out hidden from the Midianites, who have conquered and are oppressing the Israelites.

This does not appear to be a very courageous stance on Gideon's part. But when the Angel of the Lord shows up, his first words to Gideon are, "The Lord is with you, mighty warrior." Obviously, God sees something in him that Gideon doesn't see in himself. This is confirmed as the story goes on.

The Lord says to Gideon, "Go in the strength you have and save Israel out of Midian's hand. Am I not sending you?"

Gideon's response is roughly equivalent to, "Are you talking to me?" He goes on to remind the Lord that he is from the weakest clan in his tribe and that he is the least in his own family.

114

The Lord's response is, "I will go with you...." I can almost see God's smile as he's saying this. He's thinking, "This is going to be fun!" And it was!!

This is how God loves to partner with us to defeat the giants and overcome the obstacles that would stand between us and the destiny and inheritance that is ours. He faces these things with great joy and supreme confidence. We should, too, because He is in us and we are in Him. We are overcomers! We are STRONG!

It is my fervent hope that when you find yourself in circumstances that tempt you to respond out of fear, this song will empower you to face your circumstances with a joyful expectation of a victorious outcome — following a really exhilarating experience of the Lord's presence in the circumstances!

-Bob Book

GOD IN PLAIN SIGHT

Many of my prophetic words have not been words at all. They were secreted away in every day objects, one of God's favorite hiding places. He did it with Jeremiah at the Potter's House. He turned Moses' rod into a miraculous wonder, and Jesus used a fig tree to illustrate His teaching. There's a great deal of revelation in the world around us. We just need His eyes to see it.

The first time I remember encountering this was almost thirty years ago when I first moved to Yosemite. I unexpectedly landed an amazing job working at The Ansel Adams Gallery, a family-owned business that continues today. Though not a photographer myself, I loved learning about the process and history of Ansel's amazing black and white photographs.

There was one that I was particularly drawn to, without knowing why. It was an original print that hung in my office, and I never tired of looking at it. One day, I was talking with a member of Ansel's family, and they told me the story behind the photograph. It was the pivotal image that not only made his career but also revolutionized how photographs were made.

And this all occurred for one reason: Ansel took a photograph that didn't exist…except in his imagination.

"Monolith: The Face of Half Dome" is a picture that contains both a large granite rock face and a bright blue sky. In a black and white photograph, each of these elements have the same gray scale, so they blend together. To create contrast, Ansel used a red filter to cancel the blue of the sky — something that had never been done before. He underexposed the shot to preserve the detail in the snow and did several other things that broke the rules of photography at that time. He did it because snapping the shutter was the beginning of the process for him, not the end of it.

The straight print of this picture is horrible; it looks like a complete mistake. But Ansel was delighted with it. He disappeared into the darkroom, where the crafting process began. Working with the image he could only imagine, he manipulated equipment and chemicals until the sky was jet black and the huge granite face of Half Dome took center stage. Every inch of snow showed its variations and detail. What emerged from his process was a masterpiece that remains one of the most valuable photographs in history.

As my friend finished the story, I realized that God was depositing a powerful truth in me. His process of development was a great deal like Ansel's picture: when I've often only seen mistakes, He has actually allowed events to unfold that have become the perfect preparation for the masterpiece He's creating. When I've wanted to see how my circumstances could ever have a purpose, He's kept the lights of revelation turned out while He's continued to work — not because He was being unkind, but because He knows that to illuminate the truth prematurely will stop the very process needed for development.

Every time the lights go out in my life with God — during times where events seem to have no apparent reason or connection to a good outcome — I look up at the copy of Ansel's photograph that now hangs on my office wall at home and remind myself: I'm in the darkroom. There is a masterpiece in my life that's being developed even though, in the current moment, it may seem like all of my expectations have been broken and that I'm drowning in the swirl of my circumstances. My job is to remain at rest in the hands of the Master, knowing that He will finish the good work that He began in me (Philippians 1:6), and to not rush the necessary process. Intentionality (in these times) is choosing to be still and wait.

Common items, artwork, and daily occurrences can hold prophetic revelation about who we are, who we are becoming, and about the process that God will take us through on our journey with Him. When an object or incident captures your attention, take the time to "go down to the Potter's House" (Jeremiah 18:1-4) and spend some time listening to what God has to show and tell you. Write it down. Meditate on it. Continue to ask questions.

No one actually *needs* a prophetic word, but we all *need* a living, dynamic relationship with Jesus. Far too often, if I don't do a familiar form of prophetic ministry from the platform when I'm speaking at a conference, there are people who seem disappointed. They'll approach me after the session. "I was hoping to hear a word from the Lord," they sigh. With kindness, I point out that they just did—for the past hour or more! Some folks get it, but many still walk away looking sad, captive to feelings of loss that they need not have. Talk about the devil being a thief.

We want our dialogue with God to become a lifestyle, not an occasional event limited to narrowly defined prophetic occasions. He's talking to us in our Inheritance Words, our promises, with friends, and in the world around us. And we're becoming champions at hearing Him.

TOOL #4:
ADVENTURE DAYS WITH GOD

Living life on purpose can be delightfully fun and full of adventure. At times, God hides the unexpected behind a regular day that can suddenly open up into a Heavenly surprise party. Days like these can be as simple as running into an old friend at the grocery store who has the perfect insight or encouragement for you. Other days may include just looking up to suddenly be overwhelmed by the beauty of a sunset, or greeted by the smile of a child who gives you a handmade gift. I have a long list of times when God took a normal day and turned it into a treasured encounter.

But there is also the art of intentionally allowing space for wonderful things to happen. These have become my "Adventure Days" with God.

The first teaching I heard by Graham Cooke introduced me to the concept of "Adventure Days" (though it was far from his main point). In his classic teaching, *Why Wounded and Betrayed Believers are Useful to God*, he talks about having a free day during a ministry tour. He asked God what He wanted to do. Did He want to stay in the room and chat, or go exploring around the town? After discussing it for a while, the plan for the day eventually unfolded: to delightfully wander the city together, in search of a particular, extravagant item. Once it was found, Graham purchased it, and carried it back to England. It would later become a powerful prophetic word and symbol for one of his dear friends during a crucial point of life.

My first experience with this teaching radically impacted my life for many reasons beyond this story. It was a powerful teaching on God's redemptive nature, no matter what our circumstances and it completely changed how I viewed times of adversity. So it wasn't until many weeks later, after listening to the cassette tape countless times, that I was captivated by something that I hadn't really considered before: Graham went *shopping* with God. How did I miss that?

The concept of doing something in everyday life with God (as you would with any other friend) amazed me...and I couldn't wait to try it. I set aside a day the following week to go to the Sierra Nevada mountains with God: no agenda, no real plan (or so I thought), just time with my Friend.

When the day arrived, I filled my daypack with supplies, threw in my journal, and started driving. The high country was about an hour or so from my home, and I left early in the morning. I had no expectations of anything spectacular but was just enjoying being immersed in the awareness of His presence and of His delight in me.

While this first Adventure Day would prove to be different, many of my Adventure Days have remained in this presence and delight realm. These are the most common for me, and are filled with the joy of simply being with God and of living intentionally aware of Christ in me. Often, I receive no great messages or revelations—although I expect He makes deposits that He will draw on later. But I always return from each of them restored and refreshed by my fellowship with Him.

On this first Adventure, however, I had driven about twenty minutes, soaking in the beauty of the morning, when I heard His clear, inner voice say, "Let's go to Bodie." Though I had no great rush of feeling His presence, I also had no doubt Who had spoken. But—Bodie? Of all places, why Bodie?

Bodie, California, is an old gold mining town located on the eastern side of the Sierras, about sixty miles beyond where I had intended to drive. It was extremely familiar to me, because our out-of-town guests often requested to go there. Bodie's unique charm lies in the fact that it has not been restored or commercialized. Instead, it's been preserved in an arrested state of decay, with the buildings and all that is inside of them left exactly as they were when the town was abandoned. I like Bodie, but I've been there so many times that it was the last place I was thinking of going with God. I was pretty sure He would enjoy majestic mountains and alpine lakes far more than an out-of-the-way state park. Little did I know that this was His version of class was in session and I was about to begin learning some of the lessons that Adventure Days were meant to teach me.

Lesson #1:
God happily ignores our agenda for Adventure Days.
So don't bother making a formal list or having informal expectations.
He won't pay attention to either one.

God was kind enough right from the beginning to teach me that Adventure Days aren't governed by my rules or assumptions. They are delightful times to practice sensitivity and obedience with joy.

As my drive progressed, I waited for more direction (better known as "reasons that feed my need for understanding"). I would come to learn that Adventure Days are never an issue of trying to hear God, but rather of just enjoying the day with Him—trusting that, if He has something to say, He will. Details and explanations are rare. He did not confirm His word by speaking to me again, because He didn't need to. He had given me a simple enough direction, and it was my choice whether to do it or not. I also had a sense that He was fine with whatever decision I made. I felt no pressure from Him to get it right, and no fear of making a mistake. My Adventure Day was becoming a game of Follow the Leader, and an opportunity to consider a new aspect in any decision-making process:

Lesson #2:
Don't just count the cost of going. Count the cost of *not* going as well.

In the end, my ultimate decision to obey and go to Bodie was rather pragmatic. I figured that if it turned out that I hadn't heard God, it would only cost me some time and gas money. But if it was God and I didn't go, I might miss something wonderful.

So, I rolled down the windows, enjoyed the drive, stopped for lunch, cruised up the long dirt road to Bodie, and paid my entry fee to the state park. I'd just found a parking spot and was starting to consider what to do next when God piped up again. "Go to the cemetery."

Lesson #3:
If explicit directions are going to be given,
they will usually be given *as* you go — not before you get there.

Obedience can be like a long hallway of progressive doors. One door leads to another door, which leads to another door, and to another after that. Often you won't know what's behind the last door in that hallway until you've walked through all the ones before it. Adventure Days are times to practice that dynamic of obedience on a smaller scale, without the pressure of swirling circumstances that might surround you in a more urgent situation. These days allow your spirit to embed more of that process into your soul, so that, when the true challenges of life are happening around you, you can remember what it was like to respond to "Follow Me."

And, this day, obedience required going into the cemetery at Bodie, which was great. I love old cemeteries. History has always intrigued me, and the stories that can be found on old grave stones are often remarkable. I couldn't wait to see what life-changing message was written on one of those stones for me.

But the first markers were far from encouraging. They included death by gun fight, death by bar brawl and death by hanging. The next row began with the sad little markers of babies and children. It wasn't just that I felt uninspired, but I was progressing quickly towards being depressed. Maybe I had heard wrong? Maybe "cemetery" was really "elementary," and I was supposed to go to the school house? Could God have developed a speech impediment?

Just when I was ready to walk away (and probably while some poor angel was rolling his eyes), I looked up and saw a large marker at the very back of the cemetery. "That's it!!!" The Spirit shouted so loud inside of me that I jumped. "That's what I brought you here to see!"

On the very edge of the burial ground, high on the hill, was a large stone cairn, cemented together. On it was a smooth granite plaque that read:

"Near here, on July 20, 1859, Waterman Bodey, along with his partner and his burro, struck gold. Four months later, returning with supplies, he lost his life in a blinding snowstorm. This strong, indomitable man left Bodie to posterity, never knowing what he had discovered."

The last words seemed to raise off the stone: *"...**never knowing what he had discovered.**"*

And then I heard God's loving whisper.

**"Finding isn't enough.
You'll need to know how to endure if you want to finish well."**

That day, I sat for a long time on that windswept hillside by the cairn, deeply considering Waterman Bodey, the indomitable man who, as it turned out, wasn't so indomitable after all.

I'd included a guidebook for the Sierras in my pack, so I flipped to the section on Bodie and began to read. Waterman Bodey had come to California in the initial Gold Rush of 1849. He spent the next ten years searching for gold, and like many others, had found nothing. Eventually, he made his way to this remote area of the eastern Sierras to explore where no one else had even considered looking...and he found gold. But Bodey didn't just find a gold strike; he found a Mother Lode. His discovery turned out to be one of the richest deposits ever uncovered in California, proving to be worth over $34 million dollars during the next fifty years.

The vast size and value of his discovery wasn't the only thing Bodey didn't know. He was also unaware that this eastern side of the mountain range had an entirely different climate than the western Sierras he was so familiar with. The vicious winters on this side often sent temperatures plunging to -20 degrees for weeks on end. Bodey's moderate supplies soon ran out, and he was forced to brave the weather and leave his claim in order to restock. He never made it back. If he had been well-equipped, he would have still endured a very long, very boring, very cold winter—

but when Spring came, he would have been alive, ready to uncover the enormous riches that he had just scratched the surface of.

God waited for me to finish reading the story before He made a sobering statement. "You can discover a Mother Lode in ministry, and you can go forward. I will bless you and others in it. You'll see some great things." His voice then became very gentle. "But, when the winters of adversity come, you will not survive them."

He followed this statement with a question that went straight to the heart of why He'd brought me to Bodie that day. "Will you allow Me to go back into those areas—those holes of insecurity and inaccurate perceptions—and fill them with Who I really am?"

Lesson #4:
Adventure days can end up messing with your life.

God was not telling me what was wrong. He was showing me what was missing. There were gaps that I didn't even know existed, but that would make me needlessly vulnerable in the future, and He didn't want to see that happen. In the months that followed my Adventure Day, it was not always a pleasant process to view my life from His perspective, seeing just how big some of the holes were. I could have ignored their existence or covered them with a temporary fix from a How To book on spirituality. But the kindness and the freedom God offered me that day at Bodie was irresistible. He had captivated my heart with His desire for me to finish well, and it became my passion, too. The relational process to allow Him to fill those areas with Himself would need to be authentic, deep, and intentional. I quickly realized that anything else would be a cheap substitute.

Our adversary is quite content to let us get out on the battlefield, seemingly successful with our teaching, preaching, writing (whatever it is that we do in ministry)—if he knows that, one day, he can set off the time bomb that he's hidden away in our vulnerable places. He peddles cheap, quick fixes of self-improvement in hopes that we'll remain satisfied with trying harder to do better—never allowing God to complete the deep, relational process that would have displaced the bomb. Authentic Kingdom development, in partnership with the Holy Spirit, is a serious threat to the enemy and is something that he wishes to divert us away from at all costs. True transformation can only come from beholding who God really is, and everyone who pursues that process with God will eventually become like Him (2 Corinthians 3:18). That's the foundation of joyful endurance and is one of the great outcomes of an intentional life.

The day I went to Bodie, I was in a season of my life where I'd been offered some expansive ministry opportunities. Sitting in the dirt next to Waterman Bodey's grave, I realized that I faced a choice: I could continue forward, or I could place every gift and every dream back into God's reliable hands until we had supplied my life with what I would need to endure in the long run. At that moment, everything seemed to be sunny and warm in my world, but God understood that seasons change and that I was not prepared for the hard places ahead.

The missing pieces that He saw did not become a long list of the all the changes that I needed to make. *He* was the missing piece in every gap, in every weakness that I had. My journey with Him would not be an experience of trying to fix all of my "issues" but rather of coming to know Who He was for me in each of those areas. I would discover (and I continue to discover) the joy of being alive to Him in a way that I couldn't have imagined before that day.

And, because God is meticulous in His details (and His humor), He made His point in an old graveyard. We weren't going to be working to try to make the old me better. We would be discovering Who Jesus was in the new, true me, and I would be alive to Him. I later learned that Waterman Bodey's body isn't even buried in that grave. In fact, no one really knows where it is. The "Old Man" is nowhere to be found!

I've been unwrapping that encounter in Bodie for over ten years. In the months that followed my initial trip, I stepped back from further advances in ministry and spent time exploring my relationship with God. Occasionally, I would return to Bodie, and God would tell me more of our story. Sometimes when I'd go back, I would just sit and worship Him, and we would simply *be* together as we reflected on the path travelled so far and the one that lay ahead.

God chose to write the final chapter of my Bodie tale during another series of Adventure Days a few years later. It was a time in my life when God had decided that climbing mountains on our Adventure Days would be instructional for me. Most of these climbs had been presence and delight days without words. But this particular day, I found myself at the top of the most arduous ascent I'd ever done. I was looking out over the horizon, deep into the interior of the Sierras, when He said, "Turn around."

I turned and looked back across the wide open plains at the base of the mountain range. Far in the distance I saw a dark speck. It took me a while to realize that the speck was Bodie.

"Three years ago, you were sitting in that graveyard. Now, you're at the top of a mountain… That's how far you've come." His statement took my breath away, but He wasn't finished.

"And that…" He turned me back around to face the endless expanse of snow-covered peaks. "That is where we're going next: the Undiscovered Country of life with Me."

Lesson #5:
Adventure Days are worth taking… definitely worth taking!

Take an Adventure Day by walking in a park and noticing the creation around you. Go to a movie and laugh with God. And (one of my personal favorites) definitely go shopping! Days of adventure can involve a grand destination or just be an everyday event that you and God do together. Often, there is no seemingly deep meaning—just a sense of His pleasure in what you're doing together because He knows that you love doing it. My Adventure Days have ranged from a walk down the country road in front of my home to a week-long exploration of Washington D.C. and its importance at a pivotal point in American history.

A couple of years ago, God upped the ante on Adventure Days by taking me to the other side of the world to explore Australia, a country that I had never been to but that I know I have an inheritance in. At one point on the trip, I was on a small boat in rough waters where the Tasman Sea meets the Indian Ocean. The next point of landfall would have been Antarctica. I was literally at the ends of the Earth, in a raging ocean, lashed to my perch to avoid being pitched overboard—and I was having a blast. God chose that moment in time to simply whisper to me a familiar phrase from one of my Inheritance Words... and in an instant, I encountered a Truth so powerfully magnificent, that it still completely overwhelms me, even though two years have passed.

Could He have done that in my living room? Sure, He could have. But God remains a creative God, full of fun and laughter. He thought it was delightful to expand my capacity for majesty by sending me geographically farther than I had ever imagined, on an adventure He knew that I would adore. Then He set the scene to match my Inheritance Word so perfectly, that I would be overcome, not only by His majesty, but by His meticulous faithfulness to craft the delivery of the revelation with such care.

And the price of that experience? He had paid for it all. It is one of the best aspects about Adventure Days: to see how they are financed. My only role is to ask: who's picking up the bill? If it's God (and it usually is), the journey of provision is often as exciting as the trip itself. And if I'm financing it? Then, it's a cost I'm glad to pay. I've seen enough to be thoroughly convinced on that point!

It is a form of worship for us to say "These days..." or "This afternoon..." or "The next two hours are for You and me, God. What should we do?" We honor Him when He stirs a dream in our heart that we may have no idea how we will afford, but we begin to move forward in that direction. The power is found in the intentionality of making space for connection with Him. That space may be a presence and delight day that renews and refreshes you, or it could turn into something that flips your world completely. You may find yourself walking down your hometown street, seeing familiar surroundings from a new perspective, or traveling to countries that you never imagined you would see.

Adventure Days are not limited to my life or to this format. I've had a lot of people who've heard this teaching and realized that they have already been doing their own unique version of this. Others have planned an Adventure Day for the first time and have written to tell me about their wonderful explorations that included elements I have never thought of, nor experienced. I love that.

And, if you continue in this delightful exploration, you will most likely discover that somehow, while you weren't aware of it, *every* day has become an Adventure Day, filled with possibilities that you can more easily perceive because you've developed the capacity to recognize them. These eventful days have taken their place among all your days, becoming yet another facet of your continuing life with God.

TOOL #5:
STONES OF REMEMBRANCE

On the morning of the day that Israel crossed over into the Promised Land, I believe Joshua was up early—surveying the landscape, thinking about the day ahead. The last time he had walked on the other side of the Jordan River, he had been with Caleb and ten other spies, covertly exploring fruit-filled vineyards and walled cities.

That morning, he would cross into the land as the new leader of a nation that had waited forty years to occupy their inheritance.

He remembered the words of encouragement from his mentor, Moses, and from the Lord Himself: "Only be strong and very courageous..." (Joshua 1:7, NASB). That instruction had come with a promise that God would be with him wherever he went. It was a promise that Joshua knew the value of.

In Exodus 24, we find Joshua as high on Mt. Sinai as he is allowed to be when Moses first goes up to talk to God. (It's well-worth noting: Pursuing the presence of God will keep you out of Golden Calf Incidents.) Joshua was so passionate for the presence of God that he practically lived in the tabernacle, staying even when Moses would return to camp (Exodus 33:11). He adored being with God more than being seen with a great leader.

With Joshua's life focused on living in God's presence, it would seem that courage and strength would naturally result, and in many ways, they had. He aligned quickly with Caleb, who had eyes to see God's majesty in the land when the other spies saw only obstacles (Numbers 13). He led the Israeli army to victory in battle (Exodus 17) with the Amalekites, a tribe that not only occupied a portion of the Promised Land of Canaan but had also successfully attacked the Israelites from behind as they were leaving Egypt (Deuteronomy 25:17). His leadership continued to be recognized and developed as he trained with Moses (Deuteronomy 34:9).

But as the sun rose that destiny-filled morning, Moses was dead and the days of mourning for him had ended. All eyes were focused on Joshua. He had God's promises, battle plans, and the support of the Twelve Tribes. He had sent two spies into Jericho (since twelve had proved to be ten too many in his experience), and they had returned with reports of the inhabitant's terror. He gave the orders to the Israelites to prepare to finally cross over into the Promised Land.

He shared with the people how God told him it would happen (Joshua 3). They would see the waters of the Jordan part, and they would pass through on dry land. It was a rather significant manifestation of God's promise that "...as I was with Moses, so I shall be with you" (Joshua 1:5). But unlike Moses at the Red Sea, Joshua had no rod to stretch out over the Jordan River. The river would part when the feet of the priests who carried the Ark of the Covenant touched the waters. This time, the miracle would not be initiated by a sign of authority but rather by a demonstration of the power of God's presence among them.

Joshua 4 describes God's specific instructions and how each tribe was to assign a man to gather a large stone from the dry riverbed as they crossed. After they had arrived at the opposite shore, the stones were to be constructed into a memorial, a place of remembrance where elders could return with younger generations and share the stories of what the Lord had done, perpetuating the history of His faithfulness.

And, while a nation was focused on walking across a miraculously dry Jordan river, into their long-awaited inheritance, this new leader of a nation did something that is often overlooked.

"Then Joshua set up twelve stones in the midst of the Jordan, in the place where the feet of the priests who bore the ark of the covenant stood; and they are there to this day" (Joshua 4:9).

It's possible that very few people even saw Joshua do this. In the chaos of thousands crossing over, with everyone focused on what this moment meant for them, he could have set his stones in place largely unnoticed.

What was he doing? Or more accurately, *why* was he doing it?

There's really no way to know, but I have a thought that has stayed with me for many years. Israel was instructed to construct a memorial by picking up stones out of the river to put on the land. The purpose for that memorial was that it be seen by generations to come, so they could remember and be grateful to God.

Is it possible that Joshua took stones from the land of his inheritance in order to place them on the very spot where God's presence and fulfilled promise would make him great in the eyes of a nation? Was he building a hidden memorial of thanksgiving for where he had been and where he was about to go? A touchstone of God's many provisions on a very long journey as an encouragement for all the days ahead? I think so.

Maybe there was a stone for the day they left Egypt, and one filled with his memories of the towering walls of water as they had crossed the Red Sea forty years before. There might have been a rock to commemorate his partner-in-adventure, Caleb; maybe one was to remember the thousands of Israelites who didn't live to see that day. Was there a stone in memory of his wise mentor, friend, and champion, Moses? Or for the years of manna and clothes that never wore out? Perhaps the last of the twelve stones set was to simply say, "Thanks for *this* moment," as Joshua stood literally in the middle of a miracle, surrounded by the Presence of the One he adored.

At the moment he was being elevated in the eyes of all Israel, Joshua chose to remember the One who had kept him on that journey — and to say, "Thank You."

Truly great people, whether publicly known or privately hidden, are intentionally mindful of the Source of all that they attain. David understood and acknowledged that God's gentleness and goodness was what had made him great (2 Samuel 22:36). He understood that remembering, thanksgiving and joy are intricately connected. Over 15 different Psalms have a theme of thanksgiving, and throughout his writings, David remembers the works of the Lord as a chief form of encouragement during difficult times. One of my favorite examples is in Psalm 77:

"And I said, 'This is my anguish;
But I will **remember** the years of the right hand of the Most High.
I will **remember** the works of the Lord;
Surely I will **remember** Your wonders of old.
I will also meditate on all Your work, and talk of Your deeds.'"
(Psalm 77:10-13)

Another is Psalm 136, "Oh, give thanks to the Lord, for He is good! For His mercy endures forever." The entire psalm is a recounting of creation and a remembrance of God's faithfulness to Israel time and time again… from the man, who on his toughest days, knew how to encourage himself in the Lord (1 Samuel 30:6).

Remembering God's goodness creates thanksgiving.
Thanksgiving generates Joy.
Joy fuels us with enduring strength.

Over fifteen times in Deuteronomy, Moses told the Israelites to *remember*, everything from being slaves in Egypt to God's provision in the wilderness. In the years that would come, we read of Israel rebelling and becoming enslaved again and again, until God would raise up another judge or king to deliver them. Why? Because they "…did not *remember* the Lord their God" (Judges 8:34). They lost their sense of wonder, thanksgiving and joy — and it left them vulnerable to being overwhelmed by their enemies.

Jesus used his last meal before enduring the cross to create a moment for His disciples to remember, even though they didn't really understand it as they sat around the table that night. Jesus wasn't just eating a piece of bread with a sip of wine. His actions and His words showed them (and

131

us) how to pause and consider deeply the sacrifice of His body and His blood. He used everyday elements as a reminder that the New Covenant was now in effect (1 Corinthians 11:24-25). He would be the last Passover lamb, and through His sacrifice, all accounts were paid in full. "Do this in *remembrance* of Me" (Luke 22:19).

Intentionally remembering who God has been to us in our journey evokes thanksgiving and joy that gives us confidence for the unknown territory ahead. On challenging days, you can call a friend who shared a God adventure with you, and say, "Remember when God did...." You'll end that conversation in a different, more positive mindset than you began with. I often imagine that there was a lot of remembering around the campfire between David and his Mighty Men, between Joshua and Caleb, and amongst Peter, James and John when they happened to be in town together during their apostolic years. And a lot of thankful hearts when they considered all that God had done.

We can value our "God memories" by collecting them in notebooks, in pictures, with artwork, or even on Post-Its as part of the dots we collect. It's not the manner in which we record them that is important.

It's that they need to be recorded — lest in times of difficulty, we forget. These are your Stones of Remembrance.

It takes intentionality to remember God's goodness and faithfulness, especially under pressure. So make it easier on yourself. Surround yourself with reminders that will evoke thanksgiving and joy. My office and devotional space have a large number of items that look like simple, decorator pieces. But each one has a story that encourages me.

A basket from the fully financed, exceedingly abundant trip to Boston reminds me that what God orders, He will pay for. I often write out dreams that need financing on little scraps of paper and place them inside the Cape Cod basket that I bought on that adventure. It's my tangible way of saying, "God is faithful to take care of the resources that I both need and desire."

A B-24 compass from my father's combat plane reminds me that I will always have the direction that I need because God is my True North. It's also a reminder of His faithfulness to bring our loved ones safely home, no matter what the odds.

A pair of worn dancing shoes evokes my gratitude for the privilege of being present for the most amazing night of worship I've ever encountered, as well as for the many others I've been a part of. I hold them frequently and remember to pray, "More, Lord."

An Ethiopian bracelet that's made of shrapnel encourages me that God excels in crafting beauty from ashes.

The title and description of a bottle of wine from a dear friend stands as a statement of who I am and of who I am becoming in the prophetic. It officially christened a new year and a fresh season of my life.

My childhood copy of "Winnie-the-Pooh" keeps me focused on simplicity and the joy of being an adored daughter of God. When I open it and read my mother's inscription (written to me when I was six), I see how graciously I have been loved and cared for.

A portrait of my hero, Abraham Lincoln, hangs on my office wall. It was taken just after he'd received Grant's telegram that the war had ended. On his way back to the White House, he stopped at Alexander Gardner's photography studio for what would be the final photograph of his life. Lincoln would be dead in five days; in many ways, the last casualty of the Civil War. The faintest smile on his weary face reminds me of the cost of greatness, that God loves exalting the least likely, and that there are causes that are worth giving your life for.

Whether it's journals, photographs, or objects, my "Stones of Remembrance" surround me with constant invitations to be encouraged and inspired. Like Joshua's memorial hidden in the waters of the Jordan River, they are disguised as ordinary looking objects—but I know the stories. Over the years, it's been delightful how many visitors to our home have picked up an item and asked about it. Each question has provided an opportunity for me to share a tale that often provides specific encouragement or insight that they need; and, most, importantly, an occasion to share about the One behind the memory.

**They are constant reminders that, no matter where I travel,
I will remember Who is the Faithful Author
of all that I have experienced and of all that I will ever become.**

I often imagine Joshua returning over the years to a spot on the banks of the Jordan, where he would quietly contemplate the flowing water, knowing what lay underneath the surface. Maybe he'd go there intentionally after especially tough days, or visit whenever he happened to be nearby. I imagine him remembering the submerged stone cairn when he was far away from the river, after a battle hadn't gone so well. I believe that he returned at least once after the land was settled and occupied, just to say thanks for God's faithfulness again. The Lord had been true to His word. He had never left him, nor forsaken him.

It's a promise that God is very good at keeping.

So what are some of your stones of remembrance that you have already? Or what items might you find to commemorate your journey in the future? It can be as simple as bringing home a beautiful rock from the mountains for your garden or purchasing a piece of art that connects with an experience that you've had. I've shared this concept with friends and then invited them to a night of Divine show and tell: come for dinner and bring an object that represents something positive and memorable in your life. The concept of grown ups doing show and tell is always humorous, but it is also powerful to hear the stories of your friends and get to know more about their history with God.

Joshua 4 says that the stones that Joshua piled together "...remain there to this day" (Joshua 4:9). Since the Holy Spirit rarely includes random details in Scripture, it's an interesting footnote to Joshua's story. Memorials of thanksgiving and praise endure. Floods of adversity and tides of change can't erase them. They may not be always be visible, but they live on just the same—memories written on the tablets of grateful hearts.

EPILOGUE:
THE JOURNEY FROM SERVANT TO FRIEND

Of all the stories in the Bible, it is Moses' journey that has encouraged me the most. In exile for murder, he begins his partnership with God in great reluctance, arguing about his unworthiness to a blazing manifestation of the great "I AM" at the Burning Bush. I have always found it heartening that even a hesitant agreement with the Lord will get you started in the right direction.

We read of Moses' first tentative steps on the journey back to Egypt. We watch as his confidence in God grows with each passing plague until the miracle of Passover is experienced and deliverance comes. We travel with him to the Red Sea and discover evidence of his transformation as he follows God's instructions with no protest, even though it's the greatest pressure he has had to face so far. There's an army coming to kill him, and his so-called "friends," whom he's just led out of bondage, seem to want to do the same. Behind him is a very big, very deep body of water with no bridges or boats in sight. But Moses stretches out his rod as God says and Israel crosses to safety.

By the time we arrive with him at Exodus 33, we behold a truly different man than we were first introduced to. The Israelites are up to their usual antics (having made a golden calf because they wanted a touchable, visible deity), and God sounds like He's done trying to deal with their ridiculous unbelief. Maybe He is, or maybe He is setting Moses up for what follows next. I'm not really sure; but I do know that, when the Lord offers Moses a pretty good deal, Moses is no longer a man who is looking for the easy way out.

Exodus 33 begins with God saying that He will honor His promise to Abraham, Isaac and Jacob, bless Israel, and drive out all of their enemies — but He won't be going with them. We have no record of Moses saying anything at that time, but his most immediate response is to intentionally take his tent and move it out of the camp. He shifts away from his current community to align himself with God...and listen. His dwelling place becomes the first Tabernacle of Meeting. It is at this point in the narrative that we are told that God talked with Moses *face-to-face, as a man would talk to his friend* (Exodus 33:11).

> **With that statement, could it be that God has illustrated a New Testament relationship through an Old Testament hero?**

Moses had just finished taking dictation of the Law. But, before the Law is even enacted, God makes a point to demonstrate what He's *really* after in His relationship with man. He is looking for friends, not merely law-keepers. I see the Holy Spirit painting a picture of what is to come — a time when people choose being with God over rule-based satisfaction, material gain, or fame. The first Tabernacle is someone's home! Moses *dwells* in the presence of God, leaving only to go back to share with the people what comes of his conversations with Him, a foreshadowing of a life of habitation with God, not merely visitation at Divine moments in time.

After a while, Moses knows what he wants to say to God. "Then Moses said to the Lord, "See, You say to me, 'Bring up this people.' But You have not let me know whom You will send with me. Yet You have said, 'I know you by name, and you have also found grace in My sight.' Now therefore, I pray, if I have found grace in Your sight, show me now Your way, that I may know You and that I may find grace in Your sight. And consider that this nation is Your people" (Exodus 33:12-13).

This is a personal conversation, a "You" and "me" dialogue, with the mention of the nation inserted almost as a footnote. Moses wants to know who God will send with him — not them — and seems to ignore His earlier plan to not go at all, because it's just not an option. Moses plays the grace card, telling God that *if* he has found grace in His sight, then "...Show me Your way." I think Moses is thoroughly convinced from the multiple conversations that he's had with God in his home (his tent, his dwelling place) that he has indeed found grace in the sight of God.

**He *knows* the grace of God,
and he's willing to put the fate of a nation on that foundation—
a foundation of grace, born out of a relationship.**

Reading on, God seems to relent and says, "Okay. I'll go with you." Or perhaps the Lord was continuing to create a space for Moses to intentionally step into a different kind of relationship with Him—a relationship that put the weight on grace, not works, and on relationship instead of rules? I wonder.

Either way, Moses has no intention of leaving anything unclear. The promise of victory, prosperity, and occupation of the Promised Land means nothing to him any more. He has become a "One Thing" man, as David would express so beautifully hundreds of years later: "One thing have I desired, and that will I seek, that I may dwell in the house of the Lord all the days of my life; to behold the beauty of the Lord and inquire in His tabernacle" (Psalm 27:4). God has said He would go with them; but, since He said before that He wouldn't, Moses wants to be sure before he makes any final agreements.

"If Your presence does not go with us, do not bring us up from here..." (Exodus 33:15). In other words: "Let me be sure I have this right: You're promising to go with us? Because...if You aren't going, then I'm not going. And if I'm not going, then Israel isn't going."

In that moment, Moses has chosen his Friend and their friendship above all else.

"So the Lord said to Moses, 'I will also do this thing that you have spoken; for you have found grace in My sight, and I know you by name.'" (Exodus 33:17). This verse is truly amazing. God is negotiating the future of Israel based on a personal relationship, not on a set of behavioral rules...after He had just given them the Law! One man—a friend of God, living in grace—sets the course of a nation...which, I believe, was exactly what God wanted to set a precedent for.

But there's more! Moses knows an opportunity when he sees one. In that wonderful place of friendship, Moses pushes his favor to an incredible level. He asks for the desire of his heart—a passion that I believe had grown exponentially during those dwelling place times in the presence of God.

"Show me Your glory" (Exodus 33:18).

I think that Moses is saying to God, "You know me. Now, I want to know You...really know You. I want to see the essence of Who You are. I want to see Your face."

A thousand years later, Paul would write of a similar passion in his letters. "For my determined purpose is that I may know Him, that I may progressively become more deeply and intimately acquainted with Him, perceiving and recognizing and understanding the wonders of His Person more strongly and more clearly, and that I may in that same way come to know the power outflowing from His resurrection which it exerts over believers, and that I may so share His sufferings as to be continually transformed in spirit into His likeness even to His death, in the hope of His resurrection" (Philippians 3:10, Amplified Bible).

But here was Moses, almost 1,500 years before Paul would describe this kind of relationship—desiring to see the face of God...the same guy who not only seemingly ignored the manifested glory of the Lord in the Burning Bush, but who *argued* with it. Yeah. That guy. Except: he isn't "that guy" anymore. He entered into a relational process of development with God, and it's changed not only what he does but the very core of who he is.

I wonder if God just wanted to get a man to decide between rules or relationship...and to choose relationship? Moses could have requested that God give him a lecture on the finer points of the Mt. Sinai Law. Instead, he asks to see His face. He wants to know Him.

So, God answers Moses' request as best He can. He tells Moses that His glory (all of His goodness in full manifestation) is more than Moses can physically, humanly handle. To avoid killing Moses, God will protect him in the cleft of a rock and pass by—a different kind of Passover. But as God leaves, Moses can catch a glimpse of His glorious goodness—because a face-to-face encounter would be too much.

But wait: what happened to the God who talked to Moses "...face-to-face, as a man talks with His friend"(Exodus 33:11)? Now, He's saying Moses can't look at His face? Interesting.

I've pondered this paradox probably more than any other thought in the Bible. Like we discussed in Mindset #4, I started by panning it like gold and mining it with a pickaxe, but when it finally became clearer, it was like an explosion of dynamite...I've been sorting through it and finding treasure for almost twenty years. I have no need to convince anyone else that what I've explored is true, and what follows is not meant to be an iron-clad piece of theology. It's just my journey down the path of "What if?" and you're welcome to join me if you wish to.

What if Exodus 33:11—where it says that God talked to Moses face-to-face, as a man would talk to his friend—is a statement about the *outcome* of their relationship, not specifically about that time in the Tabernacle? It's hard to imagine that it's a comment about the meetings that have occurred in Moses' dwelling place, when just a few verses later God tells Moses that he won't survive seeing Him face-to-face (verse 20).

Fast forward with me to the end of Moses' life. We find him on the border of the Promised Land, talking with God, his Friend. He is 120 years old, and we read that he was in excellent health: his eyesight was clear, and he was a strong man (Deuteronomy 34:7). Why does the Holy Spirit go out of His way to let us know that detail? And, if Moses is so healthy—then how does Moses die? It obviously isn't because he is weak or sick. He's not translated to Heaven, because there is a body for God to bury (Deuteronomy 34:6).

What killed Moses?

What if, as God and Moses were talking on Mt. Nebo, remembering the amazing journey—laughing at the ridiculous moments, lost in the goodness of their many encounters together... What if, while they were reminiscing, God simply took a step back and gave Moses what he had asked for all those years ago?

What if God said, "Moses, turn around...and look"?

And what if, in that wonderful moment of Heaven meeting Earth, God showed him His face and the fullness of His glory — and Moses' body succumbed to the weight of all that goodness...his earthly life ended, and his eternal life began.

What if that's how Moses died?

And since we're pondering "What if?"...why did God bury Moses' body so that no one could find it? (Deuteronomy 34:6) Why did He make sure we knew about that fact too? What if, in Moses, God was showing us that the Old Man of the Law was meant to be buried by God Himself and that no man could (or should) find it? Is it possible that God was giving us a picture of what was to come — the day when there would be no veil, nothing between us...the day when Christ would annihilate that separation at the cross, and we could live in a face-to-face relationship with God.

Ephesians 2:14-18 says, "For He Himself is our peace, who has made both one, and has broken down the middle wall of separation, having abolished in His flesh the enmity, that is, the law of commandments contained in ordinances, so as to create in Himself one new man from the two, thus making peace, and that He might reconcile them both to God in one body through the cross, thereby putting to death the enmity. And He came and preached peace to you who were far off and to those who were near. For through Him we both have access by one Spirit to the Father."

God gave Moses a physical glimpse of the Promised Land that lay ahead for Israel, a land that was far beyond anything they had previously inhabited. What He also may have shown him was a type of the "Promised Land" that was to come for us all. A land of relational territory, where we can live in face-to-face relationship with God out of desire, not discipline...where we can partner together in passionate purpose with Christ in us, our hope of glory (Colossians 1:27)...where we can overcome all giants of fear, lack, oppression, and captivity that would try to steal what is already ours.

What if God hid the mystery of that New Life in the story and journey of the life of His friend, Moses? And what if an even better version of that life, now in Christ, is on offer to us today in the way God was dreaming of then?

What is possible for a people who (like Moses foreshadowed), enter into a relational, Joyfully Intentional process of development with the Friend who adores us and Whom we adore?

What would be the impact of a community of people like that on the earth: a people who lived renewed by their relationship with God and with others, no matter what was occurring? What would be the influence of a strong, vibrant Church that didn't only gather occasionally in buildings but lived life woven into the fabric of their local towns and cities, encouraging, innovating, healing and loving everyone they came into contact with? And not because they had to, but because they *wanted* to! What would be possible for Christians who took responsibility for their own brilliant lives with God, living in partnership (not dependency) with their leaders and friends for their continual growing up into all things in Christ?

Imagine a community of Christians for whom no giant of economics, sickness or evil seemed too big to be overcome because the majesty of God's true nature was a greater reality. Consider a people for whom no city walls of poverty, unemployment or poor history were so strong that they couldn't see them crumbling to His favor and grace. Their impact would not come only from words spoken, but from individual and community actions taken, in joyful relentlessness: in prayer, in faith and in practical, every day contributions that exemplified the glory of God's goodness. And they would be continually refueled and renewed by being great receivers of the fullness of God's love, loving Him in return and loving (and seeing) everyone around them as He does.

YOUR PROMISED LAND IS WAITING

Does that sound idealistic? Yes, if you work from an earthbound perspective that only considers all the obstacles and the current state of our communities and many churches. But an abundant life with God is possible, or else Jesus wasn't telling us the truth when He said "...I came that they may have and enjoy life, and have it in abundance—to the fullest, till it overflows" (John 10:10 Amplified Bible). We know that it's not a life free from challenges. This verse also talks about a thief who comes to steal, kill and destroy. Jesus was very clear that we would face adversity, "I have told you these things, so that in Me you may have perfect peace and confidence. In the world you will have tribulation (trials and distress and frustration); but be of good cheer, take courage; be confident, certain, undaunted! For I have overcome the world. I have deprived it of power to harm you and have conquered it for you" (John 16:33 Amplified Bible). That's a promise we can (and many of us have) staked our lives on. No, it's not a fairy tale or wishful thinking. It won't be free of tribulation. An abundant life in God is real. It does, however, require our joyful participation.

We have His promise that "...eye has not seen, nor ear heard, nor have entered into the heart of man the things which God has prepared for those who love Him" (1 Corinthians 2:9). It hasn't entered into man's heart—but the fullness of a brilliant life with God does live in the Heart and Mind of Christ, Who abides in us. Our quest is not "out there" but instead lies in exploring our internal territory with Joyful Intentionality—aligning our perceptions, thoughts, and actions with Who God really is and how He really thinks. As the eyes of our hearts are enlightened and our minds are renewed to see our world as He does, we begin to perceive obstacles as opportunities for God to be magnificent, and our passion brings purpose to do what He is doing.

This is how Moses' successor, Joshua and his friend, Caleb, viewed the Promised Land. They saw it through the lens of majesty. That perception impacted how they thought, what they said, and the actions they decided to take as a result. Faith-filled hearts got them to the borderlands, but active engagement in a good fight was required to occupy the land they'd been promised. They understood that they were well able to take the land in partnership with God, and that they would be required to participate in that process to do so.

There is absolutely nothing unique about my life or about my process that is not fully available to every follower of Jesus Christ. My history was one of incapacitating fear and of rabid religious performance for God and people. My old self was passive, fatalistic, and a coward. However, that person no longer lives! The transformational power of God's relentless faithfulness and love is massive.

Everything I've written about is because Christ in me has truly been my hope of glory. He graciously sent me brilliant friends and mentors that introduced me to the kindness of God, the power of love, and to the active partnership of the Holy Spirit. I am a living picture of mercy... someone that all of Heaven affectionately points to and says, "If Allison can begin to get this, then anyone can!" Mine is a continuing tale of redemption, that leaves me astonished by grace. It is indeed a road-less-travelled on days, but one that is oh, so worth pursuing.

With all my heart, I truly believe that the fullness of life with God is before you to inhabit and occupy. There is nothing in your way that God has not already made provision for.

It is a choice.

Occupy or observe?
Champion or spectator?
Relationship or rules?
It's your life. Choose well.

God's endlessly kind intentions towards us deserve our lives of Joyful Intentionality with Him.

PART 3

QUESTIONS AND CONSIDERATIONS FOR PERSONAL PROCESS

Tools for Activating
Your Provision

Individual or Corporate Resources for Setting in Motion the Joyfully Intentional Mindsets Found in Chapters 1 Through 7

What does it mean to "activate your provision"?

People don't live in a blueprint. Someone has to gather the materials, learn the necessary skills, pick up the tools, and build the house. Activating Your Provision encourages you in ways of walking forward to meet the provision that God has for the next part of your journey. These are practical ways that we can enter in and joyfully cooperate with the process of unlearning and learning new ways of perceiving, thinking, and acting in our life. These sections give you ideas and dialogue starters for building your own habitation with God, not merely renting someone else's. They are meant to be adapted, expanded, and creatively extended into an interaction with God that is uniquely yours.

Activating Your Provision is not the theoretical part of development. It is the practical, every day actions that we take as we are growing up into all things in Christ. You're not "making something happen", but actively exploring possibilities that open up space for God to interact with you as your Helper, Teacher, and partner.

Activating Your Provision takes place over weeks, even months. Each section can't be boxed into a weekly assignment or given out to be completed by the next time your group meets. If you're using this book corporately, it is an opportunity to choose which aspect of Joyful Intentionality you have a desire to explore because you can't do them all at once or get them done quickly. They can be used in any order and you can take as long as you like. There is significant overlap in the kinds of questions that are asked. That is intentional. It gives you a taste of the layers of exploration that we can pursue when we think about our thinking and develop a taste for depth and height, not only breadth.

Activating Your Provision is a tool for beholding God's truth and true nature until you become what you've been reading about in that area. The questions and the processes that you find here can also be used for many other aspects of spiritual development wherever your journey may lead you.

ACTIVATING YOUR PROVISION
"INTRODUCTION: BRIDGING THE GAP"

When you look at your destiny or what you believe that God has for you in this life, is there practical training or experiences that you need or desire? What are some possibilities to consider?

Are any of these possibilities things that you have thought of before—but decided not to do? If so, why did you choose not to pursue them? Would you make a different decision now? Why or why not?

Consider investigating one of your possibilities. Which one will you look into?

NOTE: It's a good idea not to eliminate anything based on time or money at this point. Often, we are in the habit of waiting until we have all of our provision before we are willing to go forward...when, in actuality, our provision is usually ahead of us—waiting for us to walk out and meet it. Remember to trust God's promise of Isaiah 30:21: it's okay to go forward, knowing that if you get off course, you'll hear His voice behind you saying "This is the way. Walk here." But if you're moving, it's easier for Him to be directing!

Begin a conversation about that possibility with the Holy Spirit. Ask how He sees it. Take notes.

ACTIVATING YOUR PROVISION
"MINDSET #1: THE JOY OF THE JOURNEY"

Traveling To The Next Level

Once you begin to have a picture of your journey to your next upgrade, use strips of paper to write out the steps or areas of development you see God working with you in.

Find Scriptures for each one to write on the back of it. Consider using them in meditation and in crafting prayers.

Do you have promises or prophecies for any of these?

Play around with them, putting them in an ascending order. Are there some that seem to need to happen before others? Does one appear to have more weight or be more immediate?

This may or may not become apparent. Don't force it. Just engage in a conversation with the Holy Spirit and give Him room to talk if He wishes to.

If there is an order or grouping that becomes clear, jot it down, and then put everything away in an envelope.

Pull out the envelope every few months and see if anything has changed. Are there completed steps that can be removed? Are there new ones to add? Has a different sequence become apparent, or do they remain equal parts of one process?

The purpose is not to put all the pieces in all the right places and glue them down. Their benefit comes in having a small prop that both engages you in dialogue with God and serves as a reminder to continue to revisit the conversation.

ACTIVATING YOUR PROVISION
"MINDSET #2: WHO DO YOU WANT TO BECOME?"

Utilizing Adversity to Accelerate Your Journey

Adversity is often our greatest opportunity. When we can identify the Fruit of the Spirit or the character that God is working in us, we can flip a negative situation into one that is a great gift in the process of our maturity!

Identify a current area of adversity.

Enter into a conversation with the Holy Spirit about what Fruit of the Spirit or characteristic of the nature of God that He is developing in you. Begin to ask, and keep on asking. If you don't hear immediately, remember that He enjoys the time of fellowship with you.

Once you know what God wants to develop in you, consider beginning a journal on that particular trait.

Find scriptures about it, and spend time meditating on them. Write down your thoughts and discoveries.

Record times where opposition or challenges are contributing to your growth in this area.

Be sure to also record your thanks for who you are now, as well as for who you are becoming.

Revisit your thoughts every few weeks or months. See what is transforming in your perceptions, thinking, and action.

ACTIVATING YOUR PROVISION
"MINDSET #3: THE UNEXPECTED IS TO BE EXPECTED"

Practice With What You Have

Identify something that God is developing in you. In the story of the Disciples and the Storm on the Lake, God was developing their peace and training them in how to release it. What is He currently cultivating in you?

What perceptions and mindsets are currently being upgraded?

Is there anything you are unlearning in this process? If so, what is it? And what are you learning instead? (See example below)

Look at your circumstances in the past 6-12 months. Are there times where storms in your life may actually have been opportunities to practice? Are there current challenges that may God's gracious opportunities to practice now?

A visionary without a plan or the intentionality to take action is likely to end up a daydreamer. What actual steps can you take to follow through on the training process that God has initiated? Where can you practice what you are learning and encountering? With your family? In your child's school? In your community or church? On a missions trip?

Example of practice that led to unlearning old perceptions and learning God's truth:

Shortly after my encounter with Jesus that I describe in Mindset 3, I went through some of the most difficult months of my life. During the year that followed, I still felt pretty broken but was given an opportunity to go in and encourage women in prison. I didn't feel particularly strong or gifted at the time, but my life had been so recreated by God's love that I couldn't imagine not sharing that love.

I realize now that God was looking for a way to establish both the heights and depths of His love that was, at that time, still relatively new to me. How I experienced Him with the women in prison captivated my heart. As I spoke or prayed for them, His love poured through me in such an intense way that I was continually amazed. I had been going into prison for several months when He asked me a question that rocked my world...again: "You do know that I love you like that, too?" No, I realized. I didn't.

He had completely set me up. I had reached the end of my current capacity to receive, so He sent me to a place where I could experience the intensity and power of His love. He used it as a way of getting around my own battle scars that were preventing me from receiving this level of love personally. (Such a sneaky God!) Choosing to enter that training ground with intent to share the love I had encountered so far served to open up amazing provision for establishing and expanding greater fullness of God's love in my life.

ACTIVATING YOUR PROVISION
"MINDSET #4: MINERS AND TREASURE HUNTERS"

Dig Deeper

All great revelation is simply an "X" that marks the spot to dig—not a surface truth to be passed over. Mining that revelation requires focus and perseverance, but the rewards are great.

Consider beginning a journal, notebook, or photo collection of ONE primary truth that God is highlighting for you. What is it?

If it's from a teaching: get the CD or download the MP3 and create a transcript of the section that you want to focus on. If it's from a book: copy that section into a notebook or journal, allowing additional space between lines to jot notes. If it's a Scripture: write it out from several different translations of the Bible.

Leave it where you'll see it each day.

Pick it up several times a week. Read the primary truth that sparked the idea and what you've written about it so far.

Then enter into a time of worship and thanksgiving for what you've seen so far. Ask and joyfully keep on asking God for more, knowing that it's His good pleasure to give it to you.

What **evidences of transformation** do you see in:

- Your perceptions (how you view your life and the world)?

- Your thinking? What brilliant thoughts are replacing lesser ones?

- Your behavior? What is it now your good pleasure to do from delight rather than out of discipline?

- Your faith? How has your faith grown in this exploration?

ACTIVATING YOUR PROVISION
"MINDSET #5: LIFE BEYOND THE COMFORT ZONE"

Doing Something You've Never Done Before

Albert Einstein observed that "Insanity is doing the same thing over and over and expecting different results."

Find something you've never done before and do it. Or, do something you've repeatedly tried in a different way. It is the best (and possibly only) way to obtain an outcome you have never seen.

What you do can be small or big. Just shaking up your daily routine gives you practice in living outside your previous boundaries and makes you more perceptive of God's opportunities. Like swirling gold-laden silt or chipping away the quartz from a vein of gold, it is the consistency of revisiting this truth that will reveal its riches. If you do this for several weeks (months are even better), you'll be amazed at what opens up.

What did you choose to do?

What were the obstacles you overcame?

How did God overcome them with you?

What evidences of transformation do you see in your perceptions, thinking and behavior from stepping out of your comfort zone?

What did you experience with God that you hadn't before?

ACTIVATING YOUR PROVISION
"MINDSET #6: FINE TUNING YOUR RECEIVER"

Practicing Stillness and Meditation

Choose one of Graham Cooke's prophetic soaking series CDs, such as "Becoming the Beloved," "Living the Upgraded Life, " or "Thinking with God." (These are excellent to start with because they each have six individual prophetic words that are about 5-7 minutes long, and they come with a booklet that already has each word transcribed, with processing questions to use for meditation.)

Or, if you need access to an MP3 download of a prophetic word, visit the Brilliant Book House website (www.BrilliantBookHouse.com) and download the free MP3 of "Latitude and Indulgence" that is available. (See the Resource Section at the end of the book for other options for prophetic soaking words.)

After listening to the entire word several times, choose one track or portion to focus on. Focus on this section for several weeks, even if it's for just a few minutes a day.

As you listen, consider picking out one phrase or idea that captures your attention. If you have a CD with the booklet of the transcribed words, find one of the processing questions that you want to focus on and just consider that.

Ask (and keep on joyfully asking) the Holy Spirit what it means for you.

This process allows you to practice taking in less at one time but going more deeply with it. It trains you for endurance in the truth, and it also allows more time for your personal conversations with the Spirit about what this means in your unique life and journey with Him.

How was this time of extended meditation different than previous experiences?

Were there challenges in staying with one piece of material for an extended time?

What were they?

What was your process of overcoming?

ACTIVATING YOUR PROVISION
"MINDSET #7: POWERFUL CHOICES"

Choosing with Intentionality

Consider this activation when you are confronted with a significant choice.

Spend time in the Questions for Exploration for this mindset.

Take notes on the process of making this choice—not just the outcome of the choice that was made and how you made it.

What were your upgrades this time? Were you more peaceful? More joyful? More confident?

What was the specific nature of God that produced this in you?

Describe your mindset now for approaching choices in the future.

RESOURCES
FOR FURTHER EXPLORATION

Available at **www.brilliantbookhouse.com**

Allison Bown
CD series:
"Joyful Intentionality"
"Unpacking Your True Identity"
"Secrets of a Warrior"
"Conversations with God"

Scheduling: For more information on speaking or consultation invitations, email **admin@twclass.org**.

The Warrior Class: For more information, visit **www.twclass.org**.

IGNITE Workshop: For more information on hosting a workshop in your community, **visit www.twclass.org** and click on the IGNITE logo.

 Connect with Allison Bown (rhymes with "town") on Facebook on her public page: **www.facebook.com/pages/Allison-Bown**

MORE RESOURCES THAT COMPLIMENT JOYFUL INTENTIONALITY

Graham Cooke

Books:
The Nature of God (from the "Being With God" Journal series)
Beholding and Becoming (from the "Being With God" Journal series)
Approaching the Heart of Prophecy (from "The Prophecy Series")

Teaching CDs and MP3s:
"Radical Permission 1 & 2"
"The Process Series"
"The Art of Thinking Brilliantly"
"Mind of a Saint"
"Living Your True Identity"

Prophetic Soaking CDs and MP3s:
"Becoming the Beloved"(CD with transcripts and questions)
"Favor As You've Never Heard it Before" (available on iTunes)
"Latitude and Indulgence"(Free MP3 download)

Bob Book Music (CDs and MP3s):

To listen: www.bobbookmusic.com/listen_to_music
To order: www.brilliantbookhouse.com/music-1.html

ABOUT THE AUTHOR

Author, conference speaker, and consultant, Allison Bown is director of The Warrior Class and owner of Altitude Training. Known for her practical activations, layered teaching, and engaging stories that give listeners tools for breakthrough and ample inspiration for follow through, she is also the founder of IGNITE workshops, a one-day exploration of a specific aspect of spirituality, such as "Unpacking Your True Identity," "Joyful Intentionality," or "Conversations With God."

In addition to careers in psychology and directing photographic workshops, Allison spent twenty years as a primary grade teacher at Yosemite National Park El Portal School. During that time, she also found great joy in ministering weekly to inmates and training leaders both inside and outside the walls of central California's extensive prison system as part of Aglow Prison Ministry.

Allison retired from teaching in 2010 to work with Graham Cooke in developing an innovative prayer community. With a small core of pioneers, they laid the foundation of The Warrior Class (TWC), now known for its culture of joyful, continually renewed and exquisitely trained warriors who practice on the field of prophetic intercession. Graham Cooke's ministry remains TWC's primary passion and practice ground, and TWC warriors are impacting their communities worldwide with training they've received.

In 2013, Graham officially passed the baton of ownership of The Warrior Class to Allison. Altitude Training became home to TWC and the launchpad for Allison's speaking, consulting, and resource development opportunities. Altitude and TWC are vital members of Team Brilliant, and Allison regularly collaborates with Graham, Brilliant Perspectives, and Brilliant Book House on various projects.

A native of Los Angeles, Allison studied and worked in Europe before marrying Randy Bown and making their home in, or near, Yosemite for over thirty years. When she's not writing, traveling or collaborating with TWC and Team Brilliant, Allison can likely be found hiking in a Sequoia grove near her Sierra gold rush hometown, curled up with a history book, or working on projects with Randy (a retired historic preservationist, master stone mason, carpenter, and soccer coach). She designs, he builds, and they share a creative, artistic and joyful home.